All About Evergreens

Writer	Michael Dirr
Photographer	Michael Dirr
Illustrators	Ron and Ronda Hildebrand

Ortho Books

Publisher
Robert L. Iacopi

Editorial Director
Min S. Yee

Managing Editors
Anne Coolman
Michael D. Smith

Production Manager
Ernie S. Tasaki

Senior Editor
Sally W. Smith

Editors
Jim Beley
Susan Lammers
Deni Stein

Design Coordinator
Darcie S. Furlan

System Managers
Mark Zielinski
Christopher Banks

Photographic Director
Alan Copeland

Photographers
Laurie A. Black
Richard A. Christman
Michael D. McKinley

Production Editors
Linda Bouchard
Alice Mace
Kate O'Keeffe

Asst. System Manager
William F. Yusavage

Photo Editors
Anne Dickson-Pederson
Pam Peirce

Production Assistant
Don Mosley

National Sales Manager
Garry P. Wellman

Sales Assistant
Susan B. Boyle

Operations Director
William T. Pletcher

Operations Assistant
Gail L. Davis

Administrative Assistant
Georgiann Wright

Address all inquiries to
Ortho Books
Chevron Chemical Company
Consumer Products Division
575 Market Street
San Francisco, CA 94105

Chevron Chemical Company
575 Market Street, San Francisco, CA 94105

ACKNOWLEDGMENTS

Consultants:
Dr. W. Richard Hildreth
State Arboretum of Utah
University of Utah
Salt Lake City, Utah

Dr. Robert L. Ticknor
Oregon State University
Aurora, Oregon

Photo acknowledgments:
*(Names of photographers,
designers, and locations are
followed by the page numbers
on which their work appears.
R = right, L = left,
T = top, B = bottom)*

Additional photography:
J. R. Baker: 26T
Laurie Black: l, 6, 14, 15T,
Ralph S. Byther: 24
J. A. Crozier: 26B
Josephine Coatsworth: Title
    Page, 10, 12B, 22
Richard Christman: 19, 20,
    21
Spencer H. Davis, Jr.: 29
James F. Dill: 27
Derek Fell: 8, 13B, 88
Saxon Holt: Front Cover,
    12T
Gene Joyner: 28
Michael Landis: 13T, 48R
Michael McKinley: 30, 32,
    36R, 41L, 63TL, 72R,
    85R

Kathleen Michalchuk: 5
Wayne S. Moore: 25
Jack Napton: 36L, 85L
Pam Peirce: 64R, 65TR, 70,
    82L, 84R
Susan Roth: 16, Back cover
Barry Shapiro: 9
Michael D. Smith: 15B
Vermeer Manufacturing
    Company, Pella, Iowa:
    17

Garden Designer:
Ralph Osterling
Burlingame, CA: 12T

**Public gardens
pictured:**
Great Compton Garden
Mid Kent, England: 4

Hidcote Gardens
Hidcote-Bartrum,
    Gloucestershire,
    England: 10

Nymans Garden
Handcross, W. Sussex,
    England: 11

Sissinghurst Garden
Cranbrook, Kent, England:
    12B

Ladew Gardens
Monkton, MD: 13B

Longwood Gardens
Kennett Square, PA: 15B

Musser Forests
Indiana, PA: 19

Threaves School
Castle Douglas
Dumfries & Galloway,
    Scotland: 22

Special thanks to:
Mr. and Mrs. Martin Asbra

Morris Berd

Dr. Armemen Gevjan

Insight Landscaping
San Francisco, CA

E. Greg Klassen

Pennsylvania Horticulture
    Society
Philadelphia, PA
Jane Pepper

Strybing Arboretum Society
San Francisco, CA

*Kelthane® is a registered
    trademark of Rohm & Haas
    Co.
Orthene® is a registered trademark
    of Chevron Chemical Co.
Sevin® is a registered trademark of
    Union Carbide Corp.*

Front cover:
*Evergreens make this home
cozy and inviting.*

Back cover:
*Snow decorates this young
fir, emphasizing its graceful
branching pattern.
Evergreens keep a solid
presence in all seasons.*

Title page:
*Evergreens frame the
majestic mountain view of
this garden.*

All About Evergreens

A plant for all seasons
An understanding of evergreens helps you to select trees and shrubs that will fit your landscaping needs.

Page 5

Designing with evergreens
Evergreens can be used as magnificent specimen trees or low hedges. Choose the right plant for each purpose.

Page 11

Planting and care of evergreens
Have vigorous, trouble-free evergreens by caring for them properly. Specific techniques help you to select strong plants and to grow them well.

Page 17

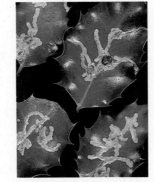

Keeping your plants healthy
Learn to control many of the pests and diseases that attack evergreens.

Page 25

Encyclopedia of evergreens
Descriptions, strengths, and weaknesses of all the great evergreens. Everything you need to know to select the right plants.

Page 31

A plant for all seasons

Evergreens are the unchanging bulwark of every garden design. An understanding of their adaptations helps you to select trees and shrubs that will be easy to care for and fit your landscaping needs.

Evergreens are the backbone of every landscape. They provide a sense of stability, strength, unity, and cohesiveness. Their appearance does not change to any appreciable degree through the seasons. In contrast, deciduous trees and shrubs are in a constant state of change: the blandness of winter gives way to the madness of spring, and the settled green of summer is followed by the riotous colors of fall.

Evergreens are trees and shrubs that hold their foliage throughout the year. *Deciduous* trees and shrubs lose all their leaves at some time in the year. Evergreens are divided into two large groups: needle and broadleaf. In the northern United States and Canada, the needle evergreens are predominant because of their cold tolerance; the most common are pine, spruce, and juniper. Broadleaf evergreens are prevalent throughout the South and the warmer parts of the West. Magnolia, eucalyptus, and cherry laurel are more frequently found in the warmer zones.

The shapes and sizes of evergreens vary widely. They range from ground covers with all types of mounds and domes to the typically pyramidal or conical, columnar, and weeping upright forms. They may be only 6 inches high, as some of the ground-cover junipers are, or soar to more than 300 feet, as the giant

Shadows of evergreens stripe a lawn, while the trees themselves unify the landscape and frame the residence.

redwoods and sequoias do. Despite their name, not all evergreens have green foliage. They may be almost white, yellow, gray, blue, bluish green, light green, or blackish green. Some species take on a bronze, purple, or muddy brown hue in winter.

Most evergreens under cultivated conditions never reach the size they do in their native habitats. Eastern white pine, for instance, has been reported to grow more than 200 feet high in New England; but grown in the Southeast or Midwest it seldom approaches 70 feet. In stands of white pine in the Southeast, some trees die seemingly without cause while others remain healthy. Stresses imposed by the heat and drought cycles probably eliminate the weaker trees. In the Midwest, needles of eastern white pine often turn yellowish because of the alkaline soils, which make iron unavailable to the plants. The trees seldom have this problem in their native eastern states because the soils there are acid.

Understanding the regional adaptability of each species is essential in planning a successful landscape. It is important to choose varieties that will thrive in your area. For example, in the area around Minneapolis–St. Paul (U.S. Department of Agriculture climate zone 4), the only broadleaf rhododendron that flowers reliably is 'PJM'. But in the Philadelphia area (zone 6), hundreds of rhododendron species and cultivars can be used. In Atlanta (zone 8), the number of large-leaf

rhododendrons that can be successfully grown drops dramatically because of the hot summers.

In general, the northern limit of a plant's adaptation is set by the winter cold. Although cold is the most important factor in limiting the region in which a species thrives, heat and humidity are also important. They are particularly important to conifers. Some of the most popular conifers are natives of northern forests.

A large fir contributes stability to this winter landscape and dramatizes the bare limbs of a deciduous white birch.

In hot-summer areas, they are weak and subject to diseases and insects that don't attack them in the North.

In the "Encyclopedia of Evergreens," beginning on page 31, we suggest both a northern and a southern limit of adaptation for many plants. The zone system we use was developed by the U.S. Department of Agriculture and is the most widely used climate zone system in this country. Because it is based on winter low temperatures, it is accurate when describing the northern limits of adaptibility of a plant but needs some interpretation when describing the southern limits. The southern limits of adaptability we describe in this book are based on the climate in the central and eastern United States, where warm summer nights are common. On the Pacific Coast, west of the Cascades and the Sierra Nevada, summer nights are usually cool, and many evergreens grow a zone or two farther south than they do in the rest of the country.

In addition to regional suitability, the size and shape of the mature plant must be considered when selecting an evergreen species for the landscape. Most evergreens grow sufficiently large to provide shade in the summer and protection from howling winds in winter. Unfortunately, many homeowners don't take into consideration the ultimate size of mature plants when designing a landscape. To the amazement of many, the cute little yew that was placed in front of the bay window 10 years ago now covers it. And the Norway spruces placed on each side of the entrance to the home have, in 15 years, threatened to push the roof from a two-story home.

It is essential to allow sufficient space for the plants to develop.

Proper plant selection will reduce maintenance and frustration in later years. The "Encyclopedia of Evergreens" provides information on plant height and spread.

Evergreens are used in landscaping for numerous reasons, both aesthetic and functional. "Designing with Evergreens," beginning on page 11, describes how they define property boundaries, enclose areas of the garden, serve as windbreaks, provide backgrounds for herbaceous plants, screen intrusive lights, drown noise, and provide privacy. Their uses are limited only by the imagination of the designer and gardener.

Leaf drop

Although evergreens never drop all their leaves (or needles) at one time, they still shed them. Needle evergreens hold their foliage for varying periods of time. The bristlecone pine (*Pinus aristata*) may hold its needles for 14 years, but the needles of eastern white pine (*P. strobus*) persist only 1 to 3 years. China fir (*Cunninghamia lanceolata*) holds its needles long after they have died, resulting in an unsightly appearance. In fact, this species often looks ragged and unkempt when it's 10 to 20 years old. In contrast, white pine is still elegant at 100 years of age.

In general, the broadleaf evergreens hold their leaves for one to two seasons. Southern magnolia (*Magnolia grandiflora*) drops its older leaves in late summer and fall, leaving only those that were produced during the spring and summer growth period. English holly (*Ilex aquifolium*) sheds older leaves in late winter and early spring. Cork oak (*Quercus suber*) drops many of its leaves in May, leading people to wonder if it is dying.

Climatic conditions sometimes determine whether a plant is truly evergreen, semievergreen, or deciduous. For example, glossy abelia (*Abelia* x *grandiflora*) in zone 8 is a broadleaf evergreen; in zone 6 it is deciduous, except for a few leaves that are held at the ends of the branches; and in zones 4 and 5 it dies back to the ground each winter and produces new growth from the base in the spring. The foliage of spreading euonymus (*Euonymus kiautschovica*) often turns brown in very cold weather (below −10° F), and the old leaves persist until the spring bud break pushes them off. But in the South, zone 7 and higher, the leaves of this tree remain rich green throughout the seasons.

In the following discussion, needle and broadleaf evergreens are described separately. The two sections also include descriptions of the aesthetics and landscape attributes of both kinds of evergreens.

Needle evergreens

Needle evergreens are woody plants whose leaves are shaped like a needle. The needles—which serve the same functions as the leaves of deciduous trees—may be flat (as in fir), quadrangular (as in spruce), or triangular, as in some of the pines. Needles vary in length from $\frac{1}{32}$ inch to 20 inches. The needles of arborvitae, false cypress, cypress, and incense cedar are so closely pressed to the stem that their true shape cannot be determined until they are pulled apart. Their foliage is termed *scale-like* because each needle so closely overlaps the other; it is generally soft to the touch. *Needlelike* foliage, on the other hand, is prickly.

The needle evergreens, particularly cone-bearing plants like the pines, spruces, and firs, were the dominant plants of the earth's first great forests. The large petrified driftwood logs found in the Petrified Forest National Monument in Arizona are the remains of an ancient forest of a now-extinct evergreen species (*Araucarioxylon*). Today, the bristlecone pine is the oldest living plant, estimated at 4000 years. Evergreens also outdo other plants in size. The giant sequoia, or big tree (*Sequoiadendron giganteum*), and the coast redwood (*Sequoia sempervirens*) are the tallest trees in

*A golden **Picea orientalis** 'Aurea Compacta' steals the show in this planting, which shows the range of form and color that needle evergreens may display.*

the world, reaching heights of more than 300 feet. But through the millenia, as a result of changes in landforms, temperature, and moisture, the numbers and ranges of evergreens have become more restricted.

Although some needle evergreens are restricted in geographic distribution, others are distributed worldwide and have adapted to almost every kind of habitat. Needle evergreens have evolved in deserts and swamps, on windswept mountaintops, and along the seashore. They are important components of the modern landscape and can survive and flourish under harsh conditions.

Needle evergreens are generally categorized as gymnosperms. *Gymnosperm* means "naked seed." At maturity, seeds of these plants are uncovered and exposed, hence naked. In cone-bearing species, the seeds lie on a cone scale and are open to view. In other kinds of gymnosperms, such as the yew (*Taxus*), the seeds are borne on a stalk and ripen in full view. The seeds of yew are covered with a fleshy red coat that ripens in October.

Although there are only about 700 species of gymnosperms living today, their contributions to human life are considerable. Of these 700 species, about 500 are conifers. In the Carboniferous period, the cone-bearing species were a major element in the swamp forests; they were transformed into coal and other hydrocarbons. Today, several pine species (western yellow pine, slash pine, loblolly pine, eastern white pine) and Douglas fir are the major timber species in the United States. They provide the lumber for our homes and offices as well as wood for furniture and other products.

Most needle-bearing gymnosperms are evergreen, with several popular exceptions. Larch (*Larix*), dawn redwood (*Metasequoia*), golden larch (*Pseudolarix*), and bald cypress (*Taxodium*) all have needle-type foliage that develops excellent fall color before dropping. All produce cones (those of the golden larch are beautiful) and are correctly referred to as *deciduous conifers*. In spite of the title of this book, you will find the deciduous conifers included.

Broadleaf evergreens

The broadleaf evergreens also retain all or part of their foliage throughout the year, but that is their only similarity to needle evergreens. Not all broadleaf evergreens have wide leaves, as their name might imply, and some plants included in the category have leaves that look like those of needle evergreens. The heather (*Calluna*) and heath (*Erica*), for example, have needlelike foliage and may remind one of a low-growing juniper. In fact, broadleaf evergreens have fine, medium, and coarse foliage textures. The heath and heather are fine; leucothoe, daphne, and barberry are medium; and cherry laurel, mahonia, and many rhododendrons are coarse.

Broadleaf evergreens are a rather heterogeneous group of plants that belong to the larger class of angiosperms. *Angiosperm* means "hidden seed," a reference to the covering (*carpel*) that encloses the seeds. There are more than 250,000 species of angiosperms, compared with 700 gymnosperm species. As a group, the angiosperms are also younger than the gymnosperms. Their evolution occurred over the past 60 million to 70 million years, compared with the ascendency of gymnosperms about 350 million years ago. Angiosperms are considered more highly evolved, and their mechanisms of flowering, fruiting, and seed dispersal are more advanced than the gymnosperms' mode of reproduction. Technically, gymnosperms have neither flowers nor fruits, most pollination being carried out by the wind. In spring, if you shake a pine tree that has male cones, clouds of yellow pollen will arise. But have you ever observed a bee, hummingbird, or beetle on a pine, savoring the nectar and facilitating pollen dispersal? Probably not. In contrast, the brightly colored and often fragrant flowers of angiosperms attract insects and birds, which in turn aid pollen transfer.

The seeds of angiosperms, including broadleaf evergreens, have several different forms. Angiosperm seed coverings may be papery, dry, fleshy, leathery, or hard. The seeds of cherry laurel, for instance, are covered by a fleshy outer coat. Holly seeds are enclosed in fleshy, almost mealy, fruit; and each seed is covered by a hard outer wall. The number of seeds per fruit, as well as their wall structure, helps to identify the species. Seeds of these broadleaf evergreens may be disseminated by birds, animals, wind, water, and humans.

Origins of Garden Evergreens

People are interested in unusual forms that deviate from the normal growth habit and foliage color. When one of these appears spontaneously, gardeners often save them. The new forms are grafted or rooted from cuttings to maintain their characteristics. They are usually named and are sold by nurseries as *cultivars* (CULTIvated VARieties). Over 200 cultivars of Norway spruce (*Picea abies*) have been named. For example, the popular bird's nest spruce is a spreading, dense, broad plant of regular growth that looks nothing like the parent Norway spruce.

Unusual forms arise in several ways. In a group of seedlings, most resemble the parent; however, an occasional seedling may grow abnormally slowly, have unusual foliage, or simply grow into a different shape. If the plant appears to have garden value, it is named and introduced as a new cultivar.

Witch's brooms—abnormally dense growth on normal trees—have been a source of many unusual dwarf conifers. These compact growths are often genetically stable, and when cuttings are rooted or grafted they maintain their compact growth habit. Some witch's brooms form cones, and the resulting seedlings show various states of dwarfness.

A third source of unusual forms is the variation that occurs in nature. Mugo pine (*Pinus mugo*), for instance, may vary from 3 to 75 feet in height. In the mountains of central and southern Europe, at high elevations, specific varieties such as *mugo* and *pumilo* are found. These are low-growing varieties that when grown from seed produce compact offspring. The commercial mugo pine varies greatly in size, due primarily to poor seed source selection. Seeds of varieties *mugo* or *pumilo* should be used to guarantee compact-growing forms. Superior compact forms of varieties *mugo* and *pumilo* have been given cultivar names and propagated by cuttings or grafting.

Bud mutations or branch sports are another source of unusual evergreens. A branch that was green in the previous growing season may produce a variegated branch as the new bud starts to emerge. If that branch is grafted or rooted from cuttings, it may grow into a variegated tree.

This Monterey cypress has been shaped into dramatic curves by the winds and rocky soil of the Pacific coast.

When they are in competition, a broadleaf species will usually dominate a needle evergreen species. Eastern red cedar, for example, is one of the first species to invade abandoned pastures or agricultural land. But as broadleaf trees become established there, they overshadow the red cedar and kill it by shading it out. Most needle evergreens are not shade-tolerant, and they become thin and unkempt in the shade. In large juniper ground-cover plantings where broadleaf trees are planted, there is usually an ever-widening ring of thin and dying juniper foliage as the broadleaf trees grow. With a few exceptions (yew and hemlock being two), needle evergreens simply do not tolerate shade.

Although they do not tolerate shade, needle evergreens tolerate other types of adversity. Many broadleaf evergreens, especially rhododendron, pieris, heather, and mountain laurel, are not particularly tolerant of adverse growing conditions. A Catawba rhododendron (*Rhododendron catawbiense*) planted in heavy clay soil on a steep slope has no chance of survival, but a Pfitzer Chinese juniper (*Juniperus chinensis* 'Pfitzerana') in the same location would prosper. Many broadleaf species thrive in the shade, and others can't tolerate hot sun. Daphne, camellia, pieris, rhododendron, and others prefer shade.

The major factor that limits broadleaf evergreens in northern climates is lack of cold tolerance. Only a few are tolerant of northern winters. In the South, on the other hand, broadleaf evergreens are so common that the term *evergreen* is seldom used to describe them.

Protection is important for broadleaf evergreens, especially in northern climates where cold winds dry out a plant in the winter months. The broadleaf rhododendrons are particularly susceptible when the ground is frozen and moisture is being lost through the leaves. The wind accelerates water loss from the leaves, and no replenishment is possible from the frozen soil. Cells eventually die, and the entire plant may turn brown. Covering the plant or otherwise protecting it from wind damage should alleviate the problem. (Winter protection of evergreens is discussed on page 21.)

Few ornamental plants are as functional and as beautiful as the broadleaf evergreens. Imagine a woodland border planted with Catawba rhododendrons. In May and June the rich pink, rose, lavender, and white display is bedazzling. The Catawba rhododendron is not simply a flowering plant, though; it also offers excellent foliage color and texture, especially when used in groupings, drifts, or masses. Many gardeners believe that a well-grown rhododendron has no equal.

Broadleaf evergreens also provide more seasonal interest than most needle evergreens. The evergreen cotoneasters, for instance, offer lovely white flowers in spring, refined leaves, and rich red fruits that often persist through winter. Bearberry, heather, holly, camellia, mahonia, firethorn, skimmia, and viburnum all offer year-round interest because of flowers, fruits, and vibrant foliage.

Many gardeners prefer broadleaf evergreens for ground cover. For sun, no plant can rival bearberry (*Arctostaphylos uva-ursi*); and in the shade, Japanese pachysandra (*Pachysandra terminalis*) is superb. For carpetlike ground cover, plants like heath, heather, sweetbox, privet honeysuckle, various cotoneasters, and Zabel cherry laurel provide an expanse of swales and hummocks. Both

Blue Rug juniper (*J. horizontalis* 'Blue Rug') and Japanese garden juniper (*J. procumbens*) tend to form hummocks near the center of the plant, thus producing a "wave in the carpet" appearance. Nursery owners have selected against the trait for forms that do not produce these mounds, and they now have available true carpet junipers.

Fragrance is often overlooked as an attribute of broadleaf evergreens. Form, line, texture, and color are the design qualities of plants; but fragrance should also be considered when selecting plants. The fragrance of daphne is sweet, delicate, and inviting; sweetbox, leatherleaf mahonia, Burkwood viburnum, Carolina yellow jasmine, and pittosporum all offer wonderful aromas. Osmanthus varieties provide fragrance in the fall and winter. Use any of these plants along walks, near entrances, or trafficked areas where passersby can savor the fragrance. As odor affects our ability to appreciate good food, so does it contribute to the garden-making process.

Broadleaf evergreens are important landscape components that work best when planted with needle evergreens and deciduous trees and shrubs. A subtle blending—considering the form, line, texture, color, and fragrance—contributes to a successful garden design.

Raising your own Christmas trees

As the cost of Christmas trees increases, and as fewer and fewer of us can go to the woods to cut our own trees, raising our own Christmas trees becomes a more attractive option. Also, there is a warm and personal aura around a tree you raised yourself. If you raised it on your own Christmas tree farm, the harvest is a reward similar to that which comes to gardeners as they collect vegetables from their own gardens. If you have used the tree for several years, it is like an old friend being once again welcomed into your home.

Your own Christmas tree farm

If you have a few hundred square feet available in a back corner of your yard, you can raise your own Christmas trees with a minimum of effort and cost. Because it takes several years for a tree to grow to Christmas tree height, you must plan and plant far in advance.

First decide on a species. It is possible to plant several, of course, but managing your farm will be simpler if the trees are all the same type. You can be assured of having a tree ready for each Christmas if they all grow at the same rate, and you will develop expertise in training the selected species as you gain experience with it. Firs, pines, and spruces are most often used, but choose any needle evergreen that you find attractive. Look in the Encyclopedia section to find a species that grows well in your region.

Buy two or three gallon-sized trees to begin your farm. Plant them far enough apart that the foliage will just begin to touch when the trees reach harvest size. Feed and water them carefully to help them grow as quickly as possible. Commercial Douglas firs, Monterey pines, and some other species are often sheared to make them dense and shapely. You can prune your trees by pinching the buds in the spring. Each pinch will make the tree more dense and will slow growth in the direction of the pinch. You can control density and shape this way, by pinching the trees two or three times each time new growth begins. If you know where you want the tree to stand in your home, you can even shape it for a corner or to fit flat against a wall.

Each year thereafter, plant another tree or two. As the first tree reaches Christmas tree size in a few years, you can harvest it and then plant a replacement tree in its vacant space.

Keeping Christmas trees fresh

If you have ever burned a Christmas tree that has been standing in your house for a couple of weeks, you were probably startled at how explosively it burned. The needles and branches contain large amounts of resin; as they dry out, they become extremely inflammable. Dry Christmas trees are dangerous in the house. But you can keep a Christmas tree from drying out just as you do a bouquet of cut flowers.

As soon as you cut a Christmas tree, place it in water. Several Christmas tree stands are available that contain reservoirs for this purpose, or you can make your own.

A simple stand can be made from a large bucket or tub. Stand the freshly cut tree in the tub, brace it in place with three or four short pieces of board cut just long enough to span the gap from the trunk to the inside edge of the tub, then fill the tub with sand. The sand will weight the tub and help to hold the tree in place. After you carry the tree into the house, add water to the tub. Replace the water as the tree uses it up. Check the water level every day; Christmas trees are thirsty and use water quickly.

This technique works only if the tree is fairly fresh. Most commercially harvested trees are cut weeks before Christmas and stored in the woods. The water-conducting vessels in their trunks dry out and will not function by the time you buy them. If the tree has not been stored too long you can sometimes get it to draw water by cutting the bottom few inches off the trunk to expose fresh wood.

Living Christmas trees

Another way to raise your own Christmas tree is to grow it in a container and move it into the house each Christmas. Nurseries sell balled-and-burlapped (B-and-B) and containerized trees that have been trained as Christmas trees.

Buy the smallest tree that will serve as a Christmas tree in your home. It will grow several inches a year, so give it room to expand. If the tree is in a fiberboard container, count on having it last for a year or two. Other types of containers will last as long as the tree fits into your house.

The warmth, dryness, and darkness of your home make a harsh environment for your Christmas tree. Don't leave it inside for more than a couple of weeks each Christmas. As the tree grows, it will become very heavy. The easiest way to move it is with a furniture dolly, or by half-dragging and half-carrying it in a sling made of a strong piece of fabric. Place the tree in a large saucer in your home, and water it carefully while it is inside. If it dries out it will die quickly. Ornaments and tinsel won't harm the tree if you are careful not to break branches.

Keep the tree in its original container, or the same size container, as long as you use it for a Christmas tree. As it becomes crowded in the container, its growth will slow, allowing it to fit in the house for a few more years. Each spring, pinch about three-quarters of the growth from the new buds. This will slow its growth and shape it. But don't remove all the new growth. Old needles will eventually die and drop off, and the tree needs to replace them. A slow-growing species, such as a spruce, can serve as your Christmas tree for many years. When it has grown too large, plant it in your yard. It will welcome being freed from its container with renewed growth, and will serve you as a landscape tree for many more years.

Designing with evergreens

Evergreens can be used in dozens of ways to accomplish dozens of design tasks, from the magnificent specimen tree to a low hedge or ground cover. Certain plants are best suited to each of these tasks, but the way they are most frequently used is not always the best way.

Throughout the ages, great gardens of the world have used evergreens for focal points and for creating a sense of order. At Hidcote in England, for example, Major Lawrence Johnston started in 1904 with a single cedar of Lebanon (*Cedrus libani*), a few beeches, and worn-out pastureland. The garden today is evidence of the genius of Major Johnston. The cedar still stands, and by virtue of its form and size dominates the surrounding 10 acres of gardens. Its spreading branches, rich needle color, and its height as it towers above all other plants in the garden make it a *specimen plant*.

A single specimen in an open expanse of lawn is stunning. Because of their striking appearance, the large needle evergreens certainly deserve specimen status. White pine (*Pinus strobus*), deodar cedar (*Cedrus deodara*), blue Atlas cedar (*C. atlantica* 'Glauca'), Canadian hemlock (*Tsuga canadensis*), and golden larch (*Pseudolarix kaempferi*) make magnificent specimen plants. Many of the weeping cultivars, including those of hemlock, white pine, European larch, false cypress, and cedar, are also excellent specimen plants.

Left: *This cedar of Lebanon dominates the landscape at Hidcote garden.* **Right:** *A specimen deodar cedar is framed by an open expanse of lawn.*

Screens

Evergreens, both needle and broadleaf, make excellent screens or barriers. A screen is a solid mass of vegetation that provides privacy from a busy street, hides views such as junkyards or the neighbor's dog pen, or simply provides an enclosure that offers sanctity from outside disturbances. Because they must be large to be effective, screens should be informal. They can bend and bow, curve and sway, but never adhere to a straight line, as hedges do. If sheared flat and level, they become imposing walls instead of soft backgrounds. In coastal areas, salt-tolerant evergreens are planted as a barrier

against windblown salts that can injure more sensitive species. Evergreen species that are tolerant to airborne salt include blue Atlas cedar, Leyland cypress (x *Cupressocyparis leylandii*), Monterey cypress (*Cupressus macrocarpa*), eastern red cedar (*Juniperus virginiana*), Austrian pine (*Pinus nigra*), pitch pine (*P. rigida*), and Japanese black pine (*P. thunbergiana*).

Groupings

In certain landscape situations, a grouping of evergreens is ideal. Three, five, or more plants are placed close together to create a small group. Arborvitae, especially Amer-

Top: *A mass planting requires little maintenance. Its variety makes it interesting.* Above: *The famous Sissinghurst garden "white room" is defined by boxwood hedges.*

Although most hedges are not a sufficient barrier to prevent someone from walking through the garden, they imply that the area is off limits.

The modern concept of hedge brings to mind a formal, neat wall of green that must be constantly pruned to keep it attractive. But the pruning must be done properly so the hedge retains its aesthetic dignity. Hedges are particularly useful where space is limited, as between the neighbor's driveway and your yard. There, a row of Hicks yew (*Taxus* x *media* 'Hicksi'), a distinct columnar form, may provide an effective and attractive boundary. Hedges, like screens, have a multiplicity of functions, but their use should be tempered.

Mass plantings

Mass plantings are often used on large commercial properties, where a hillside or slope may be covered with pines, junipers, bearberry, or cotoneaster. Because a large number of plants are used, the planting must be done carefully to avoid a monotonous, hollow feeling. Large expanses of ground-cover junipers are often planted with hollies, deciduous trees and shrubs, or irregular evergreens.

Groves

A grove is a group of trees larger than a grouping but not as dense as a mass planting. It implies the use of large evergreen trees to produce a small forest. Forests seem endless, but groves can be entered and exited easily. Groves are also amenable to underplanting with shade-tolerant broadleaf evergreens, especially

ican arborvitae, can be used in this way, with plants of slightly different sizes to provide a more natural appearance. Groupings of weeping evergreens, such as Sargent's weeping hemlock (*Tsuga canadensis* 'Pendula') and weeping white pine (*Pinus strobus* 'Pendula'), are particularly effective. A grouping can be used in a foundation planting to tie the house to the landscape, make the house appear larger, or subdue the starkness of a corner plant. Often a single upright tree or shrub is used at the corner of a house, but it would be much more effective to locate this plant away from the house slightly and plant a grouping of 'Otto Luyken' cherry laurel, Japanese holly, compact Oregon grape, Brown's Anglojap yew, or compact Pfitzer juniper around it. The grouping allows a visual transition from the tree to the lawn.

Hedges

Boxwood (*Buxus*) has been used for centuries for hedging, as have yews (*Taxus*), arborvitaes (*Thuja*), and Japanese holly (*Ilex crenata*).

A row of oriental arborvitae **(Platycladus orientalis)** *serves as a windbreak for roses and geraniums.*

azaleas and rhododendrons, and small perennial flowers.

Most residential lots don't have enough room to develop a large grove, but even a few hemlocks, false cypress, or pines can make an effective grove for a small property. Good choices for a grove are fast-growing species such as white, Scotch, and Austrian pines; Nootka and Sawara false cypress; all true cedars; and Japanese cryptomeria.

Accent plants
Sometimes particularly striking plants are used to highlight and draw attention to a part of the garden. Different foliage colors, shapes, and textures contribute to the uniqueness of an accent plant.

Perhaps the best evergreen accent plants are those that offer unique form. The weeping forms of blue Atlas cedar, Nootka false cypress, Japanese red pine, Scotch pine, Douglas fir, and eastern arborvitae are all striking. The weeping accents might be planted among boulders, along a stream, or in a large container or planter.

Blue-foliage evergreens can be effective accents if they are not overdone. When blue-foliage forms are mixed with green plantings of the same species, the line, form, and texture are similar but the color play provides additional interest.

Windbreaks
Evergreens also function handsomely as windbreaks, especially in the Midwest and Great Plains. They reduce the force of the wind, reduce

These topiary dogs were formed from **Taxus baccata erecta hillii.** *They are part of the hunt scene at Ladew Gardens, in Monkton, MD.*

heat loss from homes, control snow drift, and provide a habitat for birds and small animals. In the Midwest, the evergreens are often planted in staggered rows, three to five trees wide. This type of planting is referred to as a *shelterbelt*. Spruce and cypress are good windbreak plants; Monterey cypress is widely used for this purpose along the Pacific coast.

Windbreaks are most effective when placed at right angles to the wind. The distance that wind speed is reduced by the windbreak is determined first by height and second by

density. Some degree of protection extends downwind for a distance of 30 times the windbreak height.

Topiary
Topiary, the shaping of plants into specific forms, dates back to the ancient Romans, with whom it was a popular art form. Topiary plants can range from exquisite to comical.

Many large gardens, such as Ladew Gardens in Monkton, Maryland, and Longwood Gardens in Kennet Square, Pennsylvania, have topiary gardens created entirely from

yew. Topiary plants can take on the shapes of dogs, chairs, and every imaginable geometric form. They are interesting to look at and fun to make, but they require much care.

Topiary is usually shaped on a sturdy wire frame. These frames can be purchased through some mail-order garden suppliers, or you can make your own. Slow-growing, fine-textured evergreens, such as box-wood and yew, are planted at the base and allowed to grow through the frame. Branches are tied and pruned to conform to the shape of the frame. It takes several years to train even a small topiary. Simple shapes, such as the popular "poodle" form, can be fashioned without a frame.

An easier way to develop a topiary is to cover a wire frame with 1-inch-mesh chicken wire and pack it with sphagnum moss or a similar medium. Then plant a fine-textured vine, such as English ivy, winter creeper, or creeping fig, at its base. Shear the vine as it covers the frame. This method makes a finished topiary in a year or two and takes far less skill than traditional topiary.

Espaliers

The blank expanse of a wall can be made more interesting with ever-green espaliers. Espaliers are plants that have been pruned in such a way that they grow in a flat plane. There is scarcely a garden wall in Europe that is not covered by such a plant. In Europe, this method of pruning has been used for centuries in the devel-opment of fruit orchards, but in-creased labor costs have made it

much less practical today. However, espaliers are being used increasingly in ornamental plantings. They soften large blank walls, provide focal points in the garden, and can prove to be a fascinating and satisfying hobby.

Plants should be young and sup-ple so the branches can be bent and shaped to fit the design. Firethorns (*Pyracantha coccinea* and *P. koid-zumii*) make excellent espaliers be-cause they grow fast, have handsome foliage, showy flowers, and excellent orange or red fruit. Their branches are easily shaped and pruned. Coto-neaster, juniper, yew, euonymus, magnolia, loquat, photinia, osmanthus, holly, and camellia also make excellent espalier subjects.

To make an espalier, first decide on the shape and make a wire or wooden frame, or use wall ties or nails. Then bend the stems and branches to fit the outline. Tie them with rubber strips or soft string, and prune spurious branches. Within two or three years, the espalier will take shape and develop character. There are no established rules for creating an ornamental design, so the entire process can be rather individualistic.

Rock gardens

Of the various garden themes, the rock garden is to many the most interesting and beautiful. A rock garden uses various types of dwarf plants and is a perfect setting for extensive use of dwarf evergreens.

A rock garden is a collection or natural outcropping of rocks that is usually on a slope, but it may be

developed in a flat space. The best location for a rock garden is often a slope near the patio. Make sure that the spot gets ample sunshine. The soil should be a good loose loam, since many rock garden plants will not tolerate poor drainage. Although plant selection is largely based on personal taste, you should generally choose plants that don't grow more than 3 feet high, with perhaps 5 feet as a maximum. Proper pruning also keeps the plants in scale with the surroundings. Evergreens that are excellent for rock gardens include bearberry, paleleaf barberry (*Berberis candidula*), warty barberry (*B. verruculosa*), many cotoneasters, Burkwood daphne, rock (or garland) daphne, box huckleberry (*Gaylussacia brachycera*), candytuft (*Iberis sempervirens*), heather, heath, box sandmyrtle (*Leiophyllum buxifolium*), and mountain cran-berry (*Vaccinium vitis-idaea*).

Dwarf conifer garden

A dwarf conifer garden is something of a misnomer because the garden does not contain just dwarf cone-bearing plants. In a broad sense, it includes those plants that differ from the species in size, habit, and foliage color. A collection of dwarf conifers can be extremely interesting and beautiful, and can easily become a lifelong hobby. The garden may con-sist of a few or thousands of plants.

The easiest and perhaps best way to display dwarf conifers is in a large bed area that has an evergreen back-drop. Dwarf conifers are often planted in island beds (irregularly shaped beds scattered in the open lawn), but in a small area they tend to "drift" and appear forlorn. The Gotelli collection at the National Arboretum in Washington, D.C., makes use of island beds, but the areas are so large that one really never feels the island effect. Viewing the Gotelli collection, it becomes evident that dwarf conifer is a relative term, since there are evergreens 30 to 40 feet high. (If the species can grow to 100 feet, then is any shorter cultivar a dwarf?) Dwarf conifers offer exciting form, color, and texture that are more in scale with the modern landscape.

Bonsai

The ancient art of bonsai is practiced widely in Japan and other parts of Asia and is popular in the United States. Individual plants may be 300 to 500 years old and as valuable as any other masterpiece. The central premise in bonsai is to simulate great age through dwarfing so that plants a foot or so high have the same proportions and general outlines of mature specimens in nature. This is accomplished by restricting root space and artful pruning of branches and roots.

Arborvitae, Japanese cryptomeria, boxwood, juniper, false cypress (especially Hinoki), pine, spruce, and yew are excellent as bonsai.

As a gardening form, bonsai is not only for advanced gardeners and purists. It can be practiced by all gardeners, with satisfying results. Several good books are available in bookstores and garden centers that explain the principles.

Foundation plants

In northern gardens, virtually every foundation planting (the plants around the foundation of a house) contains several evergreens. Foundation plantings that consist of nothing but evergreens are often dull; a blend of needle and broadleaf evergreens as well as selected deciduous flowering shrubs and trees is ideal. A foundation planting should offer interesting form, texture, and color; but it is

difficult to achieve this with a single group of evergreens. A well-designed foundation planting is as much an art form as bonsai or topiary.

It is important to keep the planting in scale with the home. For instance, you would choose smaller plants for a single-story house than for one of three stories. Since most architectural lines are vertical or angular, try to select plants that have spreading or horizontal branches. Cherry laurel varieties, spreading yews, cotoneaster, spreading junipers, evergreen barberries, and viburnums are excellent for creating these lines. You can use evergreen ground covers such as Japanese pachysandra (*Pachysandra terminalis*), periwinkle (*Vinca minor*), and evergreen cotoneasters to tie the shrubs into a unified whole. Small flowering trees like dogwood, redbud, star magnolia, or crape myr-

tle can be used at the end of the house or—if there is enough room—to frame the doorways or break large expanses of brick or wood, such as between windows. But you must locate these plants a few feet away from the foundation to allow them room to spread.

The foundation planting should be carefully designed on paper. Outline the spaces under windows, by the entrance, and so on, and estimate plant sizes, textures, and colors that would blend harmoniously. Make lists of plants for given spaces, using the Encyclopedia at the back of this book and reference books (such as Ortho's books *All About Trees* and *Shrubs and Hedges*). Alternatives are often necessary because not every nursery or garden center will have just the species or cultivar you select. The process is fun, but it demands a measure of creativity and thought.

15

Above: *Dwarf evergreens are ideal for small gardens, whether you collect and display them or use them to create the backbone of a small-scale landscape. This collection shows the range of forms, from columnar* **Juniperus virginiana 'Skyrocket'** *(tall shrub at right) to rounded, golden-hued* **Chamaecyparis lawsoniana 'Leutocompacta'** *(upper left).*
Left: *A bonsai* **Juniperus procumbens 'Nana'.** *It is part of the collection at Longwood Gardens in Kennet Square, PA.*

Planting and care of evergreens

From selecting healthy plants at the nursery, to caring for mature trees in the landscape, specific techniques can help you to have the most vigorous, trouble-free evergreens possible.

Most evergreen trees that are not named varieties are raised from seed. Most named varieties are raised from cuttings. The seedlings or rooted cuttings may be planted in a field, weeded, fertilized, and trained until they are ready for sale. Or they may be planted in containers. The first container they are planted in is usually a 1-gallon can. Plants sold in this size container are known as 1-gallon plants. As they outgrow these containers, they are transplanted into 5-gallon cans, then perhaps into 10-gallon or larger containers.

Field-raised evergreens are usually sold with a ball of soil around their roots, wrapped with burlap and twine to keep it intact. They are called *balled-and-burlapped,* or *B-and-B,* plants. Since the ball of soil is heavy, these plants are seldom shipped far from where they were raised. Evergreens are usually seen in this form in northern nurseries, where cold winters make container growing difficult. But as the cost of digging and wrapping the evergreens increases, more and more nurseries are experimenting with ways to keep container plants from freezing in the winter. More container plants will probably be sold in northern nurseries in the future.

Selection of plants hardy in your area and attention to proper planting and care can create a rewarding year-round landscape.

Selecting an evergreen in a nursery

When selecting a B-and-B plant in a nursery, look first at the foliage. It should be of a healthy green color, without any visible insect or disease problems. There should be no signs of recent heavy pruning, which may be an effort to hide problems. A very flat ball indicates the root system is sparse. A large root stub protruding through the burlap indicates that there are very few small, fibrous roots. You can't unwrap the ball to inspect it, but it should be firm and unbroken. When you rock the tree, the soil ball should rock too. If the soil ball has been broken, roots have also been broken.

Most evergreens sold in southern nurseries are in containers. The foliage of container plants should have a healthy green color. If the plant is in a container with tapered sides, pull it out of its can. This can be done by tapping the rim of a 1-gallon can on a hard surface or laying a 5-gallon can on its side and rolling and tapping it to loosen the soil ball. Then slip the plant out of the can. The roots should be visible circling the inside of the can. They should be tan or brown with white tips. If a solid mass of roots hides the soil, the plant has been in that can too long and is *rootbound.* Rootbound plants have often stopped growth and are difficult to get started again.

Evergreens sold through the mail are usually shipped *bare-root.* These are small field-grown plants that

Burlap and twine protect the roots of a balled-and-burlapped Christmas tree.

have been dug up and had the soil removed from around their roots. The roots are packed in damp sphagnum moss or some other material to keep them from drying out.

Care of plants

If you can't transplant your new plants at once, place them in shade under a tree or on the north side of the house and keep them well watered. Use the sprinkler to water B-and-B plants (daily in hot weather), and fill containers with a hose.

When to plant

Container-grown and B-and-B evergreens can be planted almost any time of year except when the ground is frozen. The best time to plant is just before a time of ideal growing conditions. Since most evergreens are stressed by both summer heat and winter cold, fall and spring are the best planting seasons. In most areas, the fall planting season begins as the summer heat passes, around the middle of August, and lasts through October. The spring planting season begins as soon as the ground can be worked and continues until hot weather arrives.

In areas of the country where the winter brings drying winds, such as the Midwest and the Great Plains, evergreens subject to winter burn should be transplanted in spring so they will have as much time as possible to establish a large root system before winter.

Bare-root stock must be planted while it is quiescent and not growing, in the winter or early spring; this allows the root system to become established before top growth occurs.

The planting hole

Pick a location where the soil is well drained. The hole should be the depth of the plant's root ball, so that the root ball sits on undisturbed soil and the top of the root ball is at ground level. If the root ball is sitting on disturbed soil, it is almost sure to settle with time and watering, lowering the crown of the plant (where the trunk meets the roots) below the general soil level. Eventually, soil fills the depression around the crown. Moist soil around the crown causes *crown rot* in many species of evergreens. This is usually fatal and is a cause of many planting failures.

The hole should be about twice the diameter of the root ball or, for bare-root plants, be able to accommodate the roots when they are spread out. This space allows ample room for the roots to grow.

Amendments

Amendments such as peat moss, bark, and sand are often mixed with the native soil to be used as backfill around the plants.

Although adding amendments to the backfill is a time-honored tradition, there is no scientific evidence to support the practice. Recent research has shown no benefit from the use of amendments, and in fact showed that root growth was less in amended than in unamended soil. Many horticultural advisors now recommend that no amendments be added to the backfill. This is a dramatic change in recommendations in areas that have heavy clay or very sandy native soil. Interestingly, in tests on heavy clay, azaleas and dogwoods, which usually prefer good drainage, produced greater shoot and root growth in unamended soil.

Planting B-and-B plants

Generally, smaller B-and-B plants can be transplanted more successfully than larger ones because there are comparatively more roots to supply the aboveground portion with water and nutrients. When transplanting heavy plants, be sure to support the root ball—and never carry the plant by its stem. You may need to use a sling of canvas or burlap. When a B-and-B plant is dropped, the ball usually breaks into a million soil pieces, each of which carries a piece of broken root.

Set the plant in the hole and place soil around the base and side to hold it in place. Then remove the rope or nails from the top of the root ball. If the covering material is natural burlap, fold it back and under so that it will be buried completely when the hole is filled. Synthetic coverings, which won't disintegrate in the soil, should be removed. The top of the root ball should be at ground level or an inch or two above it. Now add the backfill soil until the hole is filled; then make a raised rim of soil about 4 inches high around the plant to form a watering basin. The basin should have about the same diameter as the planting hole. Fill the basin with water. It isn't necessary to tamp the soil, since the natural settling of the wet soil fills air pockets and stabilizes the plant. If the plant settles, raise it by gently rocking it or placing a shovel under the root ball and applying a slight upward pressure while the basin is full of water and the backfill soil is soupy. Repeat it on opposite sides until the plant is at the desired level and stands straight. Remove rocks and large clods and give the basin its final contours.

Planting container plants

Have the nursery cut straight-sided metal cans for you if you intend to plant within a day or so. If you are going to keep the plants in containers for a while before transplanting, the cut containers make watering difficult. Cut them yourself with tin snips when you are ready to plant.

Dig the same type of hole described for B-and-B plants. Remove the plant from the container and cut the roots that are circling the outside of the root ball; make three or four vertical slashes about an inch deep. This pruning causes new roots to begin growth at each cut and keeps the roots from choking the trunk as it grows. Root pruning is the most important step in container planting. Not freeing the roots may cause poor growth, or even death.

From this point follow the procedures outlined for B-and-B plants. Container-grown plants are particularly susceptible to drying out because of the lightweight, coarse-textured planting medium. The garden soil they are planted in is usually finer than the container mix and can draw water out of the root ball.

One special kind of container plant is the large specimen plant. If the plant is in a 15-gallon can, follow the directions above but don't remove the entire can. Instead, cut the bottom out of the can with a hatchet and place the plant in the hole with the sides of the can still around it. The handles on the can make the plant easier to manipulate, and the can keeps the heavy root ball from breaking as it is moved. Cut the can sides away from the root ball after the plant is positioned in the hole.

Very large trees are sold in boxes. Trees of this size usually require heavy equipment to handle. If the construction of the box permits it, remove the bottom of the box and lower the tree into the hole; then take apart the rest of the box.

Planting bare-root plants

Bare-root plants must be protected during the planting process. The exposed root system is particularly fragile, and exposure to even an hour of sun can kill the roots.

Before planting, examine the root system and prune broken, twisted, and dead roots. Plant the tree with the crown of the plant at ground level. Spread the roots out and add backfill soil, working it between and around the roots with your fingers. Continue the process until the plant is stable and standing upright. Continue filling the hole; then build a basin and fill it with water. Most bare-root evergreen plants are small and do not require staking.

Water

Water is essential to plant life. More landscape plants, evergreen and deciduous, are injured or die because of water-related problems than for any other reason.

The soil that surrounds a plant's roots are a reservoir for water. You should fill that reservoir whenever it begins to dry out. How long you will be able to go between waterings depends on a host of factors, including the plant, the weather, and the soil. For instance, sandy soils require more frequent watering than clay. But don't try to water by the calendar, since the need for water changes too much. Plants use more water as they grow and as the season changes from spring to summer. The need for water slowly declines through the summer into fall.

When watering evergreens, it is essential to soak the soil around the plant as deeply as the plant roots penetrate. You can assume that most of the feeder roots are in the top 4 feet of soil. Light or shallow watering is actually harmful, since the small feeder roots will then develop in the moist upper 1 or 2 inches of soil. In times of drought, these shallow roots are subject to injury.

Too little water causes the youngest and tenderest leaves to wilt, then die. If the soil remains dry for long periods, older leaves or needles die, beginning with the tip or outer edge. If the plant isn't watered then, it will drop enough leaves so that it will die.

Overwatering can kill plants by reducing oxygen in the soil. Plants don't transport oxygen through their circulatory system as animals and people do. Each plant part must absorb oxygen from its environment. If air can't enter the soil because it is full of water, the feeder roots die and are unable to take up water even though the soil is sopping. The top of the plant shows the symptoms of a plant that is suffering from drought, but the symptoms usually progress more quickly, with branches dying from the tips inward in a few days or weeks. These symptoms are sometimes seen also in plants that were initially planted too deeply. Constantly wet soil also contributes to the development of root rot, which kills small roots and causes the same symptoms.

An evenly moist, well-drained soil is the best preventive against plant damage. Evergreens need water at all times of the year, although they need less in fall and winter than in spring and summer. Water broadleaf and needle evergreens thoroughly in fall. Try to have the soil as wet as possible when it freezes.

Roots of these Douglas firs are protected with a gel that conserves moisture during shipment and immediately after the trees have been transplanted.

Fertilizer

The roots of large trees and shrubs extend through hundreds of cubic feet of soil, underlying much of the garden, and many gardeners do not pay particular attention to fertilizing those plants. But sometimes they do not receive the nutrients they need. By the time deficiency symptoms are obvious, the plant has been growing slowly for a long time and valuable growth has been lost. Fertilizing evergreens is particularly important to produce rich foliage color as well as rapid growth. Also, plants that are not properly nourished are more susceptible to many diseases and insects than healthy plants are.

Unless you have had your soil tested and know which nutrients are deficient in it, feed your plants with a complete fertilizer. Complete fertilizers are those that contain the three major plant nutrients: nitrogen, phosphorus, and potassium (often abbreviated as NPK—the letters are the chemical symbols of the three elements). The percentages of these nutrients are written on fertilizer package as three numbers separated by dashes: 10–10–10, 5–10–5, 8–8–8. To calculate the amount of actual nitrogen in a complete fertilizer, multiply the percentage times the weight of the bag. A 50-pound bag of 10–10–10, for example, would contain 5 pounds of actual nitrogen (50 pounds × 0.10 = 5 pounds).

Follow application rates on the package label, or use 2 to 4 pounds of nitrogen per 1000 square feet annually. For larger evergreen trees, figure 0.1 pound of actual nitrogen per inch of trunk diameter. Thus, a 10-inch-diameter tree would need 1 pound of actual nitrogen. To convert pounds of actual nitrogen to pounds of fertilizer, divide the pounds of nitrogen needed by the percentage of nitrogen in the fertilizer. If you are using 5–10–10 fertilizer: 1 ÷ 0.05 = 20 pounds of fertilizer.

Fertilizer is best applied from October through late spring. Nitrogen stimulates lush top growth, so fertilizer applied in summer or early fall may start a new wave of growth that won't have time to harden off by winter. Adding fertilizer in October helps because the aboveground parts have hardened and are not capable of additional growth, but the roots are still active and take up the nutrients. This internal fertilizer reservoir is

shunted into the emerging spring buds and results in dramatic growth increases. Fertilizer can be applied more than once each year. You might apply half in October and the rest in midspring. This split application results in more efficient fertilizer economy and plant growth.

Broadcast the fertilizer evenly over the surface of the ground under shrubs and within or halfway beyond the *drip line* (the width of the spread of the branches) of large evergreen trees. Do not place granular fertilizer on the foliage or near the trunks of shrubs or trees. Water the entire area thoroughly after application. Plant roots cannot absorb dry fertilizer, so the nitrogen, phosphorous, potassium, and other essential growth elements must be dissolved and diluted with water.

If fertilizer is not diluted with enough water, or if too much fertilizer is applied, the plant can be damaged. The fertilizer is a salt, and salty soil can keep the plant from absorbing water. This causes leaves to wilt or become necrotic (browned) along their margins. The best way to correct overfertilizing is to leach with clean water. It is always better to apply a lower rate of fertilizer and follow with a second application than to overdo the first application.

Many evergreens are susceptible to iron *chlorosis* (yellowing of the leaves), especially when grown in alkaline soil where the iron in the soil is chemically unavailable to the plants. You can acidify the soil to free the iron by adding sulfur and aluminum sulfate. But this is a laborious and often expensive process. Iron deficiencies can most easily be corrected by using a fertilizer that contains *iron chelates* (a form of iron that isn't bound to alkaline soils). Iron fertilizers can also be sprayed directly on the foliage for the most rapid absorption. Follow the directions on the product label.

Pruning

Pruning is useful at planting time to remove dead roots and branches and to balance the top with the roots. If the top is too large in comparison with the roots, it may have a greater water demand than the root system can supply. Branches can be removed without destroying the structural integrity of the plant. But evergreens, even newly planted ones, do not need to be pruned as much as deciduous trees. On older plants, pruning is done to remove dead wood and to control size and shape.

Most large evergreen trees require minimal pruning. If left to

their own devices, they make shapely trees. For pines, the new *candles* (the expanding buds) should be cut back when the needles are about half the normal length. New buds form at the bases of some of the remaining needles, thereby ensuring a dense, compact plant. This procedure is standard for Christmas tree production. Firs, true cedars, and spruces can be treated in the same way. False cypress, Leyland cypress, juniper, yew, and arborvitae are usually pruned just before a period of rapid growth, when the pruning cuts will be covered quickly; but they can be pruned any time of the year.

Some broadleaf evergreens make flower buds in the summer that remain dormant until early the following spring. If these plants are pruned in the winter, many of the flower buds will be removed. It is almost sinful to prune Catawba rhododendron in late winter or early spring, since this effectively removes all the flower buds. But other evergreens, such as glossy abelia (*Abelia* x *grandiflora*), flower on new growth. These should be pruned in the winter or early spring to stimulate as much new growth as possible. Observe an evergreen you wish to prune to see if it blooms on old wood in early spring or on new wood in late spring or summer. Don't prune any evergreen much after late July or early August, or the new foliage that develops won't have time to harden off before winter.

Hedges are often pruned incorrectly, with the top wider than the bottom. The wide top shades the bottom of the hedge, which gradually becomes thin and open. Hedges should be wider at the bottom than at the top. This is especially important on parts of the hedge that are in the shade for part of the day and aren't receiving enough light anyway.

Prune large-leafed hedges, such as English laurel, with hand pruners instead of shears. Shears cut leaves in half, giving a chopped-up look to the hedge. For an informal hedge with a soft, billowy look, prune with hand pruners, removing half the foliage every year. This will create a denser, more feathery appearance. The more formal your hedge, the more important it is to keep it trim and square. If

Rhododendrons need only small amounts of fertilizer.

you are shearing a formal, flat-topped hedge, use a piece of string stretched between two stakes as a guide for the corners.

Mulching

Mulches generally benefit plants. They reduce water loss, prevent weed growth, maintain even soil temperature, prevent compaction, and look good. Mulches may reduce the soil temperature by 30° when the surface soil is 100° F, thus allowing roots to grow all the way to the surface. Mulches also prevent the soil from cooling off in fall, thereby aiding root growth. In spring, when air temperatures fluctuate greatly, a mulch keeps the soil temperature more uniform, reducing the possibility of early growth that might be injured or killed by late freezes.

The best and most attractive mulches are usually organic, such as bark, ground corncobs, pine needles, leaves, grass clippings, salt hay, sawdust, and material from a chipper. These materials weather to a soft gray color after a year or so and blend in with the needles, leaves, and twigs that drop out of the tree. Rocks, gravel, and crushed brick can also be used. They make a more permanent mulch but must be cleaned occasionally. Black plastic prevents water loss and stops weed growth, but it is not attractive or long-lasting.

Mulches can be applied at any time, but to do the most good they should be applied before weed growth begins and before summer droughts. Although the depth of the mulch depends on the texture of the material, a depth of 2 to 4 inches is a good rule of thumb. Organic mulches will have to be replenished every year as they break down. Mulches are especially effective on shallow-rooted evergreens like yew, boxwood, rhododendron, and pieris that resent root disturbance. The mulch also protects the root system from hoes and other cultivation equipment.

Staking

Staking is seldom needed for evergreens. Large pines, spruces, firs, and other top-heavy evergreens may, however, require staking or guying after transplanting. Even if the wind is not strong enough to blow the tree over, rocking of the tree in the

ground breaks newly formed feeder roots and prevents the tree from becoming established in the native soil. But don't stake the tree unless you need to. Staked trees don't develop as strong a trunk or root system as unstaked trees.

Winter protection

In the northern states, many needle and broadleaf evergreens benefit from winter protection. Evergreens suffer from too much sun and desiccating winds that dry out the leaves when the groundwater is still frozen, snow and ice that accumulate on the branches and cause breakage, and the alternate freezing and thawing cycles that actually push small plants out of the ground.

In winter, evergreens continue to lose water through their leaves. Water loss is greatest when the wind is high and the sun is bright and warm. Water continues to be absorbed by the roots to replenish that lost through transpiration; but if the soil is frozen or if there is limited soil water, the cells die. Then the entire plant may die. Rhododendrons, mountain laurel, and hollies are particularly susceptible to this type of

injury. These plants should be shielded from wind and partially shaded. Burlap screens can be built around the exposed evergreens, or the plants can be loosely wrapped in burlap, leaving the top and bottom 12 inches open for air circulation. Small, newly transplanted evergreens can be protected by placing four stakes around the plant, wrapping burlap on the outside, and lightly packing with oak leaves. A cylinder of fencing may be stuffed with leaves to shield a small plant.

Antidesiccants (chemicals that prevent plants from losing water) are also used to protect evergreens in the winter, with varying degrees of success. They are sprayed on the evergreens in fall and form a continuous covering over the leaves to reduce water loss. Unfortunately, they may not be effective over a long period, and many of the products on the market give varying results.

The north and east sides of a house are often more suitable for evergreens in northern latitudes because of the shade and wind protection. Leaves exposed to full winter sun become almost 20° F warmer than the air temperature. When a cloud passes overhead, there is a rapid temperature drop in the leaf tissue and some cells die. Over time, the foliage becomes brownish from the cumulative effects of dying cells. American arborvitae is very susceptible to this type of injury. Many other evergreens show a similar type of foliage discoloration in winter. Broadleaf evergreens often perform best in north, northeast, and northwest exposures because the summers are relatively cool and leaf temperatures don't fluctuate as much.

Boxwoods, yews, upright junipers, and many broadleaf evergreens in foundation plantings are subject to damage from snow and ice accumulating on the branches or cascading from the roof. Plants may be tied with string to keep them from pulling apart. This is often done with boxwood in the northeastern states and arborvitae in the West. Shelters can also be fashioned by putting two large boards in an inverted V configuration over the plants. Structures resembling small tables can also be placed over the plants.

Mulching can prevent heaving of small plants out of the ground as a result of repeated freezing and thawing. Placing mulch over frozen ground prevents thawing during winter. The mulch should be applied after the ground freezes in fall; it can be removed in the spring after the ground has permanently thawed.

Propagating evergreens
Plant propagation is the art and science of reproducing plants by seeds, cuttings, or grafts. As an art it is as old as agriculture, and as a science it is as new as today.

Seeds
Growing evergreens from seed is easy and richly rewarding. Seeds should be collected when ripe, normally in the fall, and can usually be sown immediately. Cones of spruce, fir, pine, and other conifers should be collected before they open completely. If they are allowed to fully ripen on the tree, they will shed their seeds. Collect cones when the scales are just starting to crack. Dry them on a piece of paper at room temperature so they will release the seeds. The seeds can be stored in a plastic container at 33° to 45° F for long periods. Red pine (*Pinus resinosa*) seeds stored for 30 years have been known to produce vigorous seedlings.

Yew and podocarpus seeds should be collected when the fruit is ripe, as indicated by color. The red or reddish purple coverings of yew and podocarpus indicate ripeness. The red fruits of bearberry, cotoneaster, and skimmia and the orange or red seed coats of magnolia and euonymus indicate the seeds are ripe. Fruits of broadleaf evergreens like rhododendron, heath, heather, pieris, and leucothoe must be watched carefully. The capsules (fruit) will split at maturity, and tiny seeds will be dispersed by wind and rain. Collect these fruits when they are changing from yellow-green to brown and before cracks are evident at the top of the capsule. Place the fruits on paper in a warm room and turn them every day for a week or two. Small dustlike seeds will be released. Store them like conifer seeds.

For many fleshy seeds, such as magnolia, barberry, cotoneaster, holly, and skimmia, the fruit wall (fleshy part) should be removed, since it often contains a germination inhibitor. This is easily accomplished by rubbing the fruits or seeds over a screen or placing them in a blender containing water. Mask the blender blades with heavy tape to prevent chopping the seeds into bits. Dry and store the seeds. In an experiment with southern magnolia seeds, it was found that cleaned seed (without the red seed coat) had a germination rate of about 95 percent, compared with about 5 percent of those with the seed coat intact. An inhibitor in the seed coat prevented germination. The extra effort involved in cleaning the fruits is always a smart investment.

Germination techniques
Once the seeds are cleaned, they can be either planted or stored. Many evergreen seeds are sown outside in the fall in prepared soil; germination takes place in the spring. Some seeds require a certain amount of winter chilling before germination can take place. For most conifer and broadleaf evergreen seeds, the dormancy can be satisfied by normal winter temperatures. Thus fall planting ensures reasonable germination in spring.

Seeds can also be given an artificial cold, moist period to satisfy their chilling requirement. First mix them with moist peat, sand, or vermiculite, about two to three times the volume of seed. Put the seed mix in plastic bags and label the bags. Then place the bags in the refrigerator (the vegetable crisper is best). After 2 to 3 months, remove and sow the seed mixture. Germination will take place in 2 to 3 weeks. Time the chilling so that you plant in late winter or early spring.

Other evergreen seeds, particularly heath, heather, candytuft, mountain laurel, leucothoe, pieris, and rhododendron, require no special pretreatment because they have no pronounced dormancy. Sow them on milled sphagnum moss, without covering; water and place them in a plastic bag out of direct light until they germinate. When two or three true leaves develop, transplant the young seedlings.

If in doubt about the seed germination requirements of a particular plant, it is always wise to provide

Evergreen seedlings get their start in a growing frame that can be covered in cold weather.

The striking color of these southern magnolia seeds shows that they are ripe.

a short chilling period (2 to 4 weeks). This cold period may not be absolutely required, but it usually does no harm and can actually hasten and unify seed germination.

Cuttings

Most of the shrubby and low-growing needle evergreens and almost all broadleaf evergreens are grown from cuttings. A cutting is a piece of the plant, usually a piece of stem with a leaf or two attached, that is treated so that it produces roots and becomes a new plant. Propagation from cuttings offers an advantage over seed propagation in that every plant is exactly like the other. This type of plant is called a *clone*.

As discussed previously, seed-grown plants show variations in habit, foliage, fruit, and other characteristics. For example, *Rhododendron catawbiense* 'Nova Zembla' is a cold-hardy, beautiful red-flowered form. Cuttings collected from this plant and rooted will produce plants exactly like the parent. However, none of the plants grown from 'Nova Zembla' seed will resemble it in habit, flower color, or cold-hardiness. Cuttings are usually classified as softwood, semihardwood, or hardwood.

Softwood cuttings

Softwood cuttings are prepared from soft new growth. They are usually collected in May, June, and possibly into early July, depending on the species. First prepare a rooting medium. Mix 5 parts of perlite to 1 part of peat moss. Place the mix in a pot or flat and wet it; then let it drain.

Make the cuttings from the tips of branches. Cut them 4 to 6 inches long and strip the leaves from the lower half. To increase the percentage of cuttings that root, dip the cut ends in a commercial rooting-hormone powder and tap off the excess. Poke holes in the rooting medium with a pencil and place the cuttings about 2 inches into the medium.

Since softwood cuttings are so succulent, they are very tender. Cover the pot or flat with a pane of glass or a sheet of plastic film, vented just enough that condensation does not form on its underside. Softwood cuttings generally root in 2 to 4

weeks; they can then be handled as described for seedlings.

Semihardwood cuttings

Semihardwood cuttings are taken in mid- to late summer, usually after spring growth has partially matured. Broadleaf evergreens are especially amenable to propagation by this method. For example, Fraser photinia (*Photinia* x *fraseri*) will have several growth flushes during a season. Since the new leaves and stems are bright red, it is easy to determine when they mature because they lose their color. Make the cuttings the same way as softwood cuttings. They are a little tougher than softwood cuttings and can be rooted in a light, protected spot without a glass cover. Water them frequently to keep the medium moist. The use of a rooting hormone is essential; without it, rooting success may be less than 10 percent. Semihardwood cuttings are especially effective for boxwood, daphne, holly, leucothoe, pieris, rhododendron, cherry laurel, Japanese and waxleaf privet, oleander, viburnum, and others. Needle evergreens, particularly junipers, can be rooted successfully from semihardwood cuttings. The rooting time of semihardwood cuttings varies, depending on the species, but normally takes 1 to 2 months.

Hardwood cuttings

Hardwood cuttings are taken in fall or winter after all growth has ceased. Both needle and broadleaf evergreens can be rooted with this type of cutting, although needle evergreens are most commonly done this way. Several hard freezes should occur before the cuttings are taken. Arborvitae, yew, false cypress, and juniper root easily; but spruce, fir, pine, hemlock, and others are more diffi-

cult. Remove the lower one-third to one-half of the foliage. Again, a rooting-hormone treatment is important. The rooting medium should not be kept too wet. Yew hardwood cuttings can be rooted by placing them in flats containing the peat-perlite medium, setting them under the greenhouse bench, and watering occasionally to keep the medium moist. In 3 months they should have profuse white root systems.

Cuttings of many needle and broadleaf species benefit from bottom heat, which stimulates rooting. Use heating cables or mats under the rooting medium or the flats. These can be purchased at garden centers and electrical supply shops.

Grafting

The reason for grafting is largely the same as that for cuttings: to maintain certain special plant characteristics. Weeping white pine, fastigiate white pine, weeping Norway spruce, and many needle evergreens of this nature cannot be rooted from cuttings or grown from seed. First it is necessary to get a suitable root stock upon which to place the graft (*scion*). Use a seedling of the species you wish to graft. For example, use a Norway spruce seedling for grafting the weeping Norway spruce. Grow it until the stem is about ⅜ to ⅝ inch in diameter. Move these *understocks* inside in January or February, collect the scions of the desired plant, and begin grafting. Use a side-veneer graft, as shown in the illustration.

Place the new grafts in a moist atmosphere, such as a closed polyethylene tent, or wrap them in damp sphagnum peat for a week or more until the graft unions have healed. After this healing is complete, the understock can be cut off above the scion. The plant can then be moved to a larger container or into the field.

23

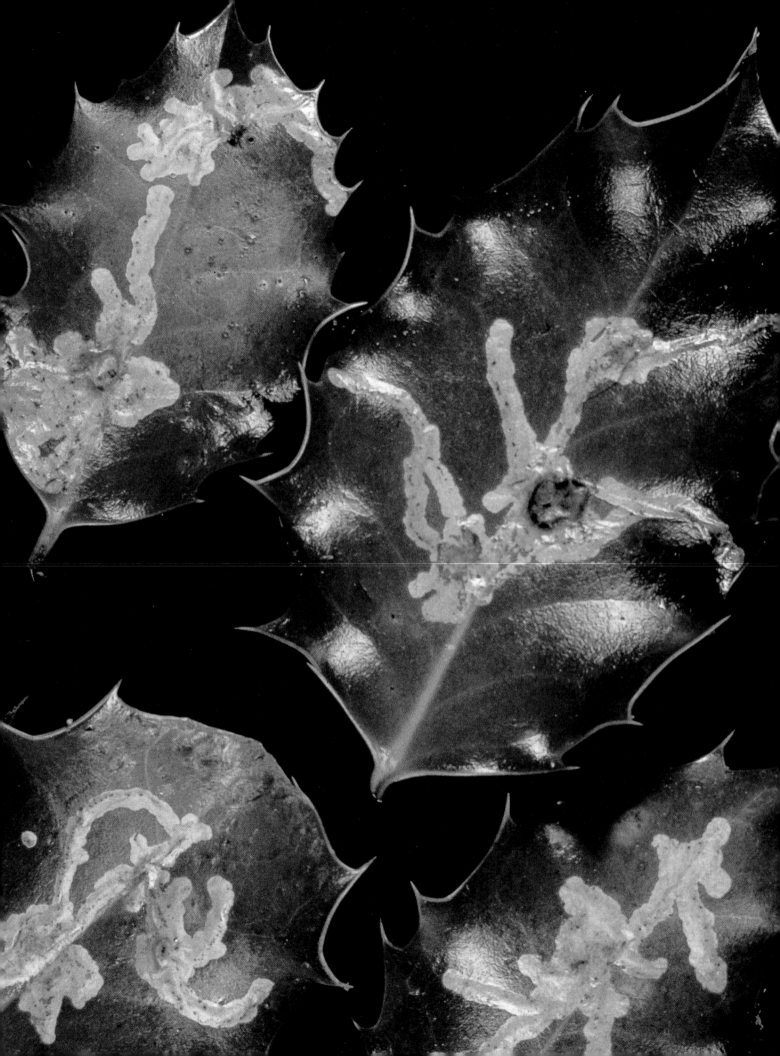

Keeping your plants healthy

Good health is the natural state of adapted evergreens. Learn to keep your trees and shrubs healthy and vigorous. Two simple rules can help you to avoid many of the pests and diseases that bother garden plants.

To the gardener, it often seems as if there is a balance between opposing forces: plants on one side and insects and diseases on the other. Gardeners often become emotional about the insects and diseases on their landscape plants. But severe control measures are not necessary under normal landscape conditions. If plants are kept healthy, and if problems are diagnosed and corrected before they become serious, the battle between opposing forces is hardly felt.

Plants in a vigorous state of growth are less susceptible to pests than plants under stress. Research has emphatically shown that plants under environmental stress are prone to insect and disease problems. Plants fight off insects and diseases with a host of chemicals that they manufacture. A healthy plant responds quickly to an invasion and repels it before it weakens or harms the plant. For instance, trees resist borers by making so much sap or pitch that the holes are filled with it and the borers drown or are forced from their holes. But weakened or stressed trees cannot manufacture pitch in the quantities needed, and are more likely to succumb to the invasion. In addition, borers are attracted to injured and stressed trees, and will often heavily infest an

Leaf miner tunnels in holly leaves.

injured tree while ignoring a healthy tree next to it.

Most plant problems start small and slowly grow serious over many weeks or even years. An alert gardener takes early measures to correct problems, while they are still easy to correct. Notice symptoms like slow growth and slight leaf discoloration, and try to find out the cause of the problem. In the East, Japanese pieris (*Pieris japonica*) is woefully susceptible to lace bug, especially when planted in a sunny location. The insect sucks the juices from the leaves and renders the plant a ghostly shade of yellow. If the insect is recognized and controlled when it first appears, the appearance of the plant can be saved.

Evergreens in general are remarkably free of serious insect and disease problems. The problems that do bother them are usually easy to identify. In fact, many insects and diseases are named according to their most common host plant, such as camellia scale, euonymus scale, and cotoneaster webworm. It's important to correctly identify an insect or disease to be able to control it. Look up the problem in *The Ortho Problem Solver,* available at a local nursery, or ask the local county extension agents for assistance. They can identify the problem and provide control recommendations. For most landscape plants, you can do any spraying that's necessary. But for large evergreen trees, it may be necessary to consult a professional arborist.

Insects
Aphids, often referred to as plant lice, are small (seldom more than ⅛ inch long) insects that suck the juice from plants. They cause distortion of the leaves and stems of many needle and broadleaf evergreens. Balsam twig aphid affects balsam fir, white fir, and spruces. Some aphids, such as the Cooley spruce gall aphid, cause galls or distortion of new growth. Balsam woolly aphid is a pest of most firs. Other woolly aphids attack larch needles and cause galls on Norway, black, Colorado, and white spruces. The pine bark aphid sucks sap from the bark of white, Scotch, and Austrian pines. Aphids also carry and transmit viruses. They

Adelgids (a type of aphid) on pine.

give off a substance called *honeydew,* a sugary liquid, which drips on leaves and objects below the tree. A fungus called *sooty mold* grows on the honeydew, making leaves black and dirty.

26

Most aphids feed on young shoots, flowers, and buds; bark and twig aphids feed on bark. They range in color from gray, green, pink, and red to black. They multiply rapidly and can ruin a plant in short order. Look for curled leaves or distorted young stems. Close inspection may reveal aphids in such numbers that the stem is not visible.

Control: A light infestation of aphids can be washed from the plant with a stream of water. Aphids are usually easy to control with insecticides, but often return in a few weeks. Use Orthene®, malathion, or diazinon, thoroughly covering the infested plant parts. Galls on spruces and other needle evergreens should be removed and burned.

Bagworms are the caterpillar stage of moths and are easily identified by the 1- to 2-inch-long bags they build from the host plant's foliage. Bagworms feed on 128 different plants, including arborvitae, 14 species of juniper, white pine, hemlock, deodar cedar, spruce, cypress, and many others. Arborvitaes and junipers are particularly susceptible; in a single season, an infestation can remove all the foliage from a large plant. Five hundred to 1,000 eggs in a single bag are common. When the eggs hatch in May or June, the larvae immediately start to construct the protective bags.

Control: Usually, bagworm infestations are not heavy and the easiest control is simply picking off the bags and disposing of them in the garbage. If infestations are heavy, spray with Orthene®, Sevin®, malathion, or diazinon before the young caterpillars build bags in the spring. Once the caterpillars are in the bags, only systemic insecticides, such as Orthene®, are effective.

Lace bugs are small insects, less than ⅛ inch long, that are seldom noticed by the gardener until after the damage has occurred. The lace bug can be identified by the lacy, netlike pattern of its wings. Since the insect feeds on the underside of the foliage, there is no immediate visible evidence of its presence. The insect sucks sap from the leaves, causing a white or yellow dotting or blotching of the upper surface. The entire plant may appear whitish if infestations are intense. Cotoneaster, firethorn, mountain laurel, pieris, and rhododendron are very susceptible. If the underside of the leaf has

brown sticky areas, it is a sure sign that lace bugs are present.

Control: Lace bug is not the easiest pest to control, since it usually stays on the underside of the leaf. Spray in May or June and again in midsummer with Sevin®, malathion, diazinon, or Orthene®, thoroughly covering the undersides of the leaves.

Mealybugs do not live through cold winters, so they are serious problems only inside and in southern areas. However, they occasionally spend the winter in greenhouses or homes in the North and cause problems outside in the summer. They appear as white, cottony masses on stems. Mealybugs are closely related to scale; they suck the sap from plants, reducing growth.

Control: Ladybugs are natural predators of mealybugs. A systemic insecticide, such as Orthene®, applied in spring or summer will control them. Malathion and diazinon are also effective.

Leaf miners are the larvae of flies, moths, sawflies, and beetles. Adults lay eggs in the leaf; and the tiny larvae that hatch from these eggs eat the interior of the leaf, leaving only the transparent epidermis. The damage may appear as serpentine tunneling or blotching, or the entire interior of the leaf may be removed. The leaves discolor, shrivel, and often fall off. Leaf miners can seriously injure holly, boxwood, pine, arborvitae, larch, and other evergreens.

Control: In the flying stage, these insects can be controlled with malathion, diazinon, or Sevin®. But once the larvae are inside the leaf (which is usually when their presence is first noticed), systemic insecticides such as Orthene® and dimethoate are needed.

Mites. Dozens of species of mites attack ornamental plants. The spruce mite and southern red mite are particularly troublesome on evergreens. The mites suck the sap from the cells, causing discoloration, stunting, and death. The injury appears as tiny yellow flecks over the leaf surface. Mite populations build rapidly in hot weather and can turn a perfectly green evergreen to yellow. To detect them, hold a piece of white paper under a branch and shake the

Spider mite webs on Italian cypress.

Pine needle scale on spruce.

branch. If tiny yellow, green, or red dots are moving about on the paper, then mites are the problem. Also, white webbing is a telltale sign that mites are feeding. The spruce mite is found only on conifers: hemlock, spruce, arborvitae, false cypress, juniper, and pine. The southern red mite is found on broadleaf evergreens: Japanese holly, azalea, camellia, mountain laurel, boxwood, rhododendron, and numerous others.

Control: Spray with a miticide, such as Kelthane or dimethoate. Mites often become resistant to a particular chemical, so it is wise to change miticides every few sprayings. Control measures should be taken at the first sign of mites, because mite populations increase rapidly and wreak havoc.

Pine-shoot moths. The larvae of moths bore through the young shoots and stems of pines, distorting and killing them. The leaders are often contorted, and the plant loses any semblance of its normal shape. The initial signs include needle yellowing, drooping tips, and resin deposits where larvae have tunneled. Christmas tree growers are constantly checking for these pests, since a serious infestation can ruin an entire plantation. Austrian, mugo, red, Scotch, Virginia, and other pine species are susceptible.

Control: Spray with a systemic insecticide, such as Orthene®, in spring or summer.

Sawflies, the larvae of nonstinging wasps, eat the mature needles of conifers. Pine, hemlock, spruce, larch, and cedar are particularly susceptible. Sawflies eat the tip of the needle first, gradually progressing to the base. If left unchecked, they can completely defoliate a needle evergreen in a short time.

Control: Sawflies are easily controlled with Orthene®, malathion, or methoxychlor in May or June.

Scales are small (less than ⅛ inch long) sucking insects that often go unnoticed until they have done considerable damage. They cover themselves with a shell of wax and cement themselves to leaves, stems, and fruits. Scale injury is manifested by reduced growth, yellow leaves, and stem dieback. Some scales produce honeydew, and leaves or objects under infested trees may be covered with a sticky liquid or the sooty mold that grows on it. These pests are found on hemlock, yew, fir, spruce, cedar, arborvitae, holly, ivy, firethorn, cherry laurel, and other species. Euonymus scale affects the winter creeper and Japanese euonymus species.

Control: Early detection and immediate measures are required to adequately control scale. Winter creeper branches can be so severely encrusted with scale that they appear white. These branches should be pruned and destroyed. Scale can be sprayed with a dormant oil in early spring. The fine oil covers the scale and causes suffocation. In May and June, when the young crawlers are moving about, spray plants with malathion, diazinon, or Orthene®.

Thrips are small flying insects that are scarcely visible to the naked eye. They suck plant sap and cause discoloration and stunting. Thrips injure both leaves and flowers. Broadleaf evergreens like euonymus, gardenia, and rhododendron are susceptible.

Control: Thrips are difficult to control, and plants may have to be sprayed every 2 weeks from spring into summer. Malathion, diazinon, Sevin®, and Orthene® are suitable insecticides.

Weevils belong to the beetle insect group. In their larval stage (called *grubs*) they live beneath the soil and feed on roots. Later, when the adult weevils emerge, they feed on foliage and may consume most of the leaf tissue except veins. Black vine weevil is particularly serious on yew, rhododendron, hemlock, and other needle and broadleaf evergreens.

Control: In June or July, spray the plants with Orthene®, making sure to give the lower leaves and stems blanket coverage.

Whiteflies are easily identified, since a cloud of small white insects appears when an infected plant is touched. The cloud reassembles on the plant if there are no additional disturbances. The adult flies are found on the undersides of the leaves, where they suck the plant sap and cause a yellowish discoloration. They produce honeydew, much as aphids and scales do.

Control: Whiteflies can be difficult to control; thorough spraying with Orthene®, diazinon, or malathion is necessary. Be sure to cover the undersides of the leaves. Repeat two or three times at 10-day intervals to kill newly hatched insects.

Diseases

Diseases of evergreens fall into two major categories: infectious and noninfectious. Fungi, bacteria, viruses, and mycoplasmas are microorganisms that infect plants, causing diseases. Noninfectious diseases are induced by environmental and cultural conditions such as nutrient deficiencies, toxicities, salt, air pollution, and excessive moisture.

All garden plants may be attacked by diseases at one time or another. There are 80,000 different diseases, so the likelihood of a plant being susceptible to one or more diseases is good. For example, 20 to 25 major disease groups (rot, leaf spot, blight, and so on) have been described for rhododendrons, with more than 20 organisms causing leaf spot alone.

Fortunately, many *pathogens* (disease-causing organisms) that cause dieback, cankers, and root rot seldom attack healthy, vigorous plants. They usually prove more serious on plants that are declining.

To successfully control plant diseases, it is necessary to correctly identify the organism. The infectious diseases described below are treated in groups to facilitate identification.

Leaf spots are probably the most common of all plant diseases; they are favored by rainy weather and high humidity. Most are not serious enough to warrant special control measures. *Fungal leaf spots* are usually well-defined spots of varying sizes, shapes, and colors. The spots may be more or less rounded and marked with concentric rings of different colors. The center is the oldest infected part; as the infection increases in size, the center may fall out, leaving a shot-hole appearance. Common cherry laurel is very susceptible to this type of injury. In recent years, entomosporium leaf spot has proven troublesome on Fraser photinia and can cause severe defoliation. *Bacterial leaf spots* are less common. They usually appear as dark, water-soaked spots on leaves and stems which later turn gray, brown, reddish brown, or black. English ivy is quite susceptible to bacterial leaf spot.

Control: For fungal leaf spots, spray captan, chlorothalonil, zineb, daconil, or benomyl when buds first break in spring. Bacterial leaf spot is harder to control; spray with streptomycin or fixed (tribasic) copper.

Blight. Needles become suddenly and conspicuously spotted; the spots enlarge and become angular to irregular in shape. Affected leaves and stems may wilt, wither, and die. Cryptomeria, cypress, daphne, Douglas fir, English ivy, euonymus, fir, giant sequoia, hemlock, juniper, larch, photinia, pine, viburnum, and other evergreens are susceptible.

Control: Use chlorothalonil or benomyl.

Mildew is manifested as a white to grayish haze over the surface of leaves, buds, young shoots, or flowers. The affected plant parts may yellow, wither, and die. It becomes prevalent in the summer months and into the fall. It is most severe in damp, shady locations where air circulation is poor and when cool nights follow warm days. Needle evergreens are not troubled with mildew to any degree, but most broadleaf evergreens are susceptible. Mildew is seldom devastating and can be readily controlled.

Control: Avoid locating broadleaf evergreens where mildew thrives. Spray with a suitable fungicide, such as triforine, karathane, chlorothalonil, sulfur, or benomyl.

Rusts are particularly evident because of the yellow, orange, reddish brown, chocolate brown, or black powdery masses that appear on needle evergreens. Most needle evergreen rusts require two kinds of plants to complete their life cycle. The most familiar are white pine blister rust and its alternate host, currant; and cedar-apple rust on juniper and the alternate host, crabapple. On white pine the rust can kill the tree. On juniper, a reddish brown, rounded gall forms during spring rains, from which orange gelatinous masses protrude. The galls do not usually hurt the juniper, but they do carry millions of spores that cause serious damage to

Fire-blight damage to loquat.

Cedar-apple rust on juniper. The alternate host of this fungus is crabapple.

apples. Juniper, spruce, pine, hemlock, Douglas fir, larch, and fir are susceptible to various rusts.

Control: Remove galls from the evergreen and burn. Spray alternate hosts with triforine, chlorothalonil, ferbam, or other suitable fungicides.

Fire blight is a bacterial disease that causes flowers and leaves to appear scorched. The stems shrink and turn brown or black. The tips of the branches are often bent to form a crook. Rapidly growing succulent parts are most susceptible to fire blight. It can prove devastating to large plantings of cotoneaster, photinia, loquat, and firethorn. The disease is spread from cankers to flowers, leaves, and young stems by insects, rain, and wind. Fire blight is active during periods of warm, humid weather. In the West, it is a spring disease; in the East, it can rage all summer long.

Control: Use resistant species or cultivars of cotoneaster and firethorn. Avoid excessive fertilization. Remove diseased stems to remove sources of spores. Fireblight can be spread by pruning tools. If the disease is still actively spreading when you prune out deseased stems, wipe the pruners with rubbing alcohol after every cut. If possible, spray fixed copper or streptomycin at 3- to 5-day intervals beginning when the first buds break and continuing through the flowering period.

Cankers. Many fungi and bacteria attack the bark of trunks and branches. The infected bark turns dark and sunken, then dies and dries up, forming a canker. The shape of the canker varies from elliptical to rounded to almost patchy. Cankers usually grow slowly for one growing season, or sometimes for more than one season. If the canker girdles a branch, it cuts off the sap flow to the end of that branch, killing it. If it girdles the trunk, it kills the tree. The best prevention is a healthy plant. Cankers do not always kill a plant but may severely weaken it. There are few evergreens that are not susceptible to canker-causing organisms.

Control: Keep plants vigorous through proper fertilization and watering. Avoid wounding plants with mowers, weed trimmers, and other power equipment. Prune out infected plant parts and burn. Between cuts, sterilize pruning shears with rubbing alcohol.

Wilts produce a general flagging or drooping of leaves and stems. Their symptoms are often confused with those of root rots, crown rots, stem cankers, drought, and other problems. The wilting is due to a temporary or permanent deficiency of water in the foliage. The three common wilts that are caused by pathogens are fusarium, verticillium, and bacterial. They affect only broadleaf evergreens. The fungi and bacteria invade the plant's sap system and plug up the vessels. The normal flow of fluids is slowed or stopped, and the wilt symptoms become evident. Cherry laurel and rhododendron are susceptible to wilt diseases. Cutting into infected stems or branches reveals discolored streaks.

Control: There isn't much you can do once the plant is infected. Promote good growth by feeding and watering carefully. Use resistant species and cultivars.

Root rots. Rot refers generally to plant tissue in various states of disintegration. Rots may be soft, wet, dry, hard, white, or black, depending on the causal agents. Improper cultural conditions, such as excessive moisture, hasten the course of the disease. Root rots are particularly hard to diagnose because they are hidden from view and easily confused with other disorders. Rhododendron and pieris may be affected by root-rot-causing organisms.

Control: As with wilts, there isn't much you can do to help the plant once rot has set in. Allow the soil to become very dry, if possible. Keep it dry as long as you can without harming the plant. Plant in well-drained soil. Avoid overwatering. If you know there are rot pathogens in the soil, sterilize it before replanting.

Crown gall. Swollen tumors or galls, often 1 to 2 inches in diameter, are usually present on stems near the soil line or on roots and stems. They are rough-surfaced, soft and spongy or hard, and greenish or dark. As the disease progresses, plants become stunted and off-color and may die. *Euonymus fortunei* is particularly susceptible to this bacterial disease, but camellia, false cypress, cotoneaster, cypress, Douglas fir, incense cedar, juniper, loquat, privet, viburnum, and yew are also susceptible.

Control: Remove infected parts and burn. Don't buy plants with suspicious swellings near the crown, soil line, or graft union. Disinfect soil with an appropriate fumigant.

Noninfectious diseases. Diagnosing these problems is often more difficult than diagnosing infectious diseases. Distinguishing a single causal factor is almost impossible because so many factors affect plant growth. For example, leaf chlorosis, or yellowing, on rhododendrons may be caused by lack of iron or manganese or by poor drainage. Before attempting remedies or control measures, limit the number of contributing factors to a minimum. (One can spray a chlorotic rhododendron all day with iron, but if it is deficient in manganese it will never turn green.)

Take samples of the damaged plant to the nursery or county agent for identification. If no answers are immediately forthcoming, ask the nursery or agent to send the samples to a state university where trained entomologists, plant pathologists, and horticulturists may become involved. Most state universities have a plant diagnostic center. Do not hesitate to ask for help. After all, as a taxpayer, you help support them.

Encyclopedia of evergreens

Many modern evergreens are greatly improved over earlier generations. Being able to choose a hardier or more graceful variety is a great advantage in selecting evergreens for the landscape.

This Encyclopedia is divided into two sections: Needle Evergreens and Broadleaf Evergreens. The entries within each section are listed alphabetically by the scientific name, which is followed by the most widely accepted common name. There are no rules governing common names, and there are many regional variations. *Pinus virginiana,* for example, is called Virginia, scrub, Jersey, spruce, and poverty pine. *Leucothoe fontanesiana* may be called drooping leucothoe, fetterbush, or dog-hobble. It is this wide variety in commons names that makes the scientific name so important. The scientific name is the name used by all people who speak or write with precision about the plant.

After the name, characteristics of the plant's foliage, such as leaf size and color, are described. If the foliage color changes significantly in the winter months, that fact is also noted.

The next bit of information in each entry is the plant's range--the climate zones where it grows best. Hardiness zones or zones of adaptability are based on the U.S. Department of Agriculture zone map (see page 96). Each zone represents an increment of 10° F. For example,

plants in zone 5 are hardy to −20° F and plants in zone 4 are hardy to −30° F. Hardiness zones are at best a guide, since they do not take into account rainfall, soil conditions, wind, and summer heat. Plants can often be grown successfully outside the recommended zones with proper care.

Following the zone data is a description of the the plant's growth rate. These rates are either *slow* (less than 12 inches per year), *moderate* (12 to 24 inches), or *fast* (more than 24 inches). So many factors affect the rate of growth that it is difficult to predict from season to season how much a specific plant will grow. However, if they are grown under ideal conditions, Leyland cypress is *fast* and bristlecone pine is *slow.*

The plant's average dimensions are provided as *height* and *spread;* both are important when choosing an evergreen for the landscape. The size given is the mature landscape size.

Finally, there is a brief description of the plant, its growing habit, and its uses in the landscape.

The scientific names given may consist of only the *genus* and *species,* or they may include a *variety* or *cultivar* name. These terms are defined below.

Genus: A large group of plants with similar flowering and fruiting structures. For example, in the genus *Pinus* (pine), all members are distinguished by the cones and the way the needles are grouped in bundles. Although cones and needles differ in

size, shape, and color, they share an inherent similarity.

Species: A group of plants with specific characteristics that are passed on from generation to generation. It is considered the most important unit of classification. Within the genus *Pinus,* for example, *Pinus strobus* (white pine) is a five-needled pine and *Pinus bungeana* (lacebark pine) is a three-needled pine.

Variety: A group of plants that grow true from seed and which in nature are often restricted to a specific geographic area. In botanical names, the term *variety* is abbreviated *var.* Within the larger group of mugo pines, *Pinus mugo* var. *pumilo* designates a group of low-growing shrubby pines from the mountains of central and southeastern Europe. Its seedlings exhibit the low-growing habit of the variety.

Cultivar: A plant that has been selected for a specific characteristic, such as foliage color, growth habit, tolerance of heat or cold, and so on. Cultivars of woody plants do not come true from seed and must be grown from cuttings or grafted. Cultivars of woody plants often occur by chance. For instance, Sargent's weeping hemlock was one of four or five seedlings found near Fishkill Landing, New York, in the 1860s that exhibited the weeping growth habit. That characteristic distinguished it from the upright habit of the rest of the species. Since then, the cultivar named Sargent's has continued to be propagated by grafting.

A profusion of evergreens, from columnar to ruglike, demonstrates the variety available.

Needle evergreens

Most of the conifers described here keep their needles all year. A few of the species listed below are deciduous, dropping their needles seasonally. Almost all the needle evergreens belong to the order Coniferales, or cone-bearing species. The only exceptions are yew and podocarpus, whose seeds are covered with a fleshy outer coat called an aril.

Abies concolor

Fir cone

Abies
The firs

Most firs grow to be large trees, often attaining a height of 100 feet or more. They range in habit from narrow and conical to pyramidal, but vary less in growth habit and needle characteristics than any other group of needle evergreens. Female cones are held upright on the upper branches of the tree and shatter at maturity, leaving a central stalk attached to the tree. The cones of several species, most notably *Abies koreana* (Korean fir), are rich purple or bluish purple before maturing to brown.

Firs are strong landscaping elements because of their vertical lines. They are best used as specimen plants or in groupings. Because of their ultimate size, they are most suitable in expansive or parklike settings where they will not overwhelm the rest of the garden.

Firs thrive in cool, humid climates and need moist, well-drained, acid soil. However, a few species, such as white fir (*A. concolor*) and Veitch fir (*A. veitchii*), do grow in drier climates. Firs require full sun for maximum growth but will tolerate light shade. Transplant firs in the spring, using balled-and-burlapped specimens. Pruning should be kept to a minimum because new growth seldom develops after older branches are removed; consequently, trees become ragged and unsightly.

In general, firs are not seriously threatened by insects or diseases under ordinary landscape conditions. However, they are not suited to urban conditions and do not tolerate smog.

Abies balsamea
Balsam fir

Flat needles, each ½ to 1 inch long, lustrous dark green, two parallel whitish bands on the lower surface.

Zones 3 to 6.

Slow growth rate.

40 to 75 feet high, 20 to 25 feet wide.

The balsam fir is commonly grown for Christmas trees but is seldom used in landscapes except where it occurs naturally. The lustrous dark green needles emit a pleasant balsam odor when bruised. The boughs are often used for Christmas wreaths and sprays.

Balsam fir makes an excellent screen or specimen evergreen in suitable climates, but it loses needles and never reaches its full potential in hot, dry situations. It is not suitable for use in smoggy urban areas.

Abies concolor
White or concolor fir

Flat needles, each 2 to 3 inches long, greenish or bluish on both surfaces, no distinct whitish bands on the lower surface.

Zones 3 to 7.

Slow to moderate growth rate.

30 to 50 feet high, 15 to 30 feet wide.

White fir is the most adaptable of all firs. It can be grown successfully in the hot, dry regions of the Midwest and upper South; but it loses color on western alkaline soils. Needles vary in color from green to rich blue ('Violacea'). Plants maintain their branches and needles to the ground, forming a dense, solid pyramid. This species is most effectively used in groupings or as an informal screen. All firs have the landscape stigma of rigid formality and may be difficult to blend into the small residential landscape.

Abies fraseri
Fraser fir

Needles similar to those of *Abies balsamea*.

Zones 5 to 7.

Slow growth rate.

30 to 40 feet high, 20 to 25 feet wide.

The Fraser fir closely resembles the balsam fir. It is used for Christmas tree production in the southern highlands, where it is found native at altitudes of 3,000 to 6,000 feet. Like balsam fir, it is not an environmentally tolerant tree and should be used only in areas that parallel the cool, moist climate of its native range.

Abies homolepis
Nikko fir

Needles about 1 inch long, lustrous dark green above, whitish bands below.

Zones 5 and 6.

Slow growth rate.

40 to 60 feet high, 15 to 25 feet wide.

The Nikko fir is a stately evergreen, appearing as a dark green pyramid in the landscape. It seems to have moderate heat tolerance and could be grown in more southerly locations if provided with light shade. Principal landscape uses are in groupings and screens or as a specimen.

Abies procera
Noble fir

Needles 1 to 1¼ inches long, dark bluish green above, narrow pale bands below.

Zones 6 and 7.

Moderate growth rate.

50 to 75 feet high, 15 to 20 feet wide.

Truly a noble fir, this tree attains its greatest stature in the West, where it is native. The needles remain attractive throughout the seasons. Noble fir requires abundant moisture and a cool, well-drained soil.

Abies veitchii
Veitch fir

Needles about 1 inch long, shiny dark green above, two conspicuous broad white bands below.

Zones 3 to 6.

Moderate growth rate.

50 to 75 feet high, 25 to 35 feet wide.

Veitch fir is a particularly attractive broad pyramidal evergreen that can serve as an effective screen or grouping. It shows reasonable tolerance to dry conditions.

Araucaria araucana
Monkey-puzzle tree

Needles 1 to 2 inches long, extremely spiny, glossy dark green on both surfaces.

Zones 9 and 10 (8 to 10 on the West Coast).

Slow to moderate growth rate.

50 to 60 feet high, 15 to 20 feet wide.

A most elegant and unusual tree, which often evokes the response "What is it?" Its growth habit is pyramidal

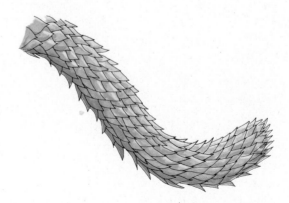

Araucaria stem tip

Left: *Calocedrus decurrens*   **Below:** *Cedrus atlantica*

to oval, with stout branches that sweep down and finally up at their extremities. Its foliage texture is so different from that of other needle evergreens that the plant can only be considered for specimen use. Soils should be moist, deep, and well drained. It grows best with a sunny exposure.

A related species, *Araucaria heterophylla* (Norfolk Island pine), with light green needles and horizontal branches, is suitable for use in zone 10. It is often planted in containers or tubs on patios in more northerly

Calocedrus stem tip

areas, but it needs indoor protection during winter. *Araucaria bidwillii* (bunya-bunya) is a columnar species with somewhat pendulous main branches.

Calocedrus decurrens
(Libocedrus decurrens)
California incense cedar

Scalelike needles overlapping on stems, creating soft fronds of lustrous rich green foliage.

Zones 5 to 8.

Moderate growth rate.

30 to 50 feet high, 8 to 10 feet wide.

This beautiful evergreen is easily mistaken for an arborvitae at first glance. Its unique columnar habit can be likened to an exclamation point, so it is a strong element in the landscape. Unless used in sufficient numbers in groupings, it appears totally out of place. If pruned, it can be used as a hedge or screen. The cinnamon-red bark develops a scaly, almost

peeling quality. It is one of the most adaptable evergreens and can be grown from Massachusetts to Georgia and west to the Pacific Coast. A moist, deep, well-drained, acid soil is most suitable. Its tolerance to heat and drought provide landscape flexibility.

Cedrus
The cedars

Cedars are a noble and distinguished group of needle evergreens. In youth they appear somewhat stiff and rigid, but with age they assume a grandeur unrivaled by any other conifer. All are large trees, and a mature cedar may cover 1,000 square feet. The needles are 1 to 2 inches long, angular, and sharply pointed. They are borne singly on the new growth of the season and in clusters on older growth. Cedars bear their candle-shaped male cones, which shed pollen in the fall, on the lower branches and their egg-shaped female

*Cedar
needle attachment*

cones on the upper branches. The female cones take 2 years to mature.

These trees are best suited to large properties such as estates, parks, and golf courses. The cedars, especially *C. deodara*, are excellent for dry-soil areas but are not particularly tolerant of extreme cold (below −10° F). Prune cedars when their new growth is hardening off. Older branches, 6 to 12 inches in diameter, can also be pruned if necessary; they will resprout.

Left: *Cedrus deodara*   Below: *Cedrus libani*

Cedrus atlantica
Atlas cedar

Needles ¾ to 1½ inches long, dark green to bluish green.

Zones 6 to 9.

Moderate growth rate.

40 to 60 feet high, 30 to 40 feet wide.

The Atlas cedar appears rather forlorn in youth because of its stiff, rather gaunt outline, but with age it assumes a flat-topped habit with horizontally spreading branches. This is possibly the most tolerant of the cedars to dry soils and air pollution, although it grows best in moist, deep, loamy soil in full sun. Needle color varies considerably, from green to blue. The cultivar 'Glauca', with rich bluish green foliage, is widely available commercially, as is the unique 'Glauca Pendula', which has similar foliage and a weeping growth habit.

Cedrus deodara
Deodar cedar

Needles 1½ to 2 inches long (the longest among the cedars), very sharply pointed, usually bluish green.

Zones 7 to 9.

Moderate growth rate.

40 to 70 feet high, slightly less in spread.

Deodar cedar is the most graceful of the cedars in youth. Its growth habit is broad pyramidal, and its branches are semi-pendulous. The top nods gracefully, giving it a characteristic silhouette. With age, it becomes wide spreading with a flat top. The bluish green needles are attractive throughout the seasons.

The deodar cedar is perhaps the most elegant conifer for use throughout the southern part of the country and westward to California. In west Texas it withstands dry alkaline soils, incessant wind, and low humidity. 'Kashmir', 'Kingsville', and 'Shalimar' are hardier forms than the species. 'Shalimar', the hardiest of the three, tolerates temperatures as low as −10° F. In the South, deodar cedar is better adapted than *C. libani*.

Cedrus libani
Cedar of Lebanon

Needles average 1 inch long, lustrous dark green.

Zones 5 to 7 (to 8 on the West Coast).

Slow growth rate.

40 to 60 feet high, similar spread.

Cedar of Lebanon is a rather unassuming tree in youth, much like its close relative *C. atlantica,* but it becomes stately with age. It develops a thick, massive trunk and wide-spreading branches, with the lower branches sweeping the ground. Its needles are generally lustrous dark green, distinguishing it from *C. deodara* and *C. atlantica* 'Glauca'. This is the hardiest species; established trees have survived temperatures of −15° to −25° F. The variety *stenocoma* is even hardier but more stiff and rigid than the species; and in old age it never assumes the wide-spreading outline.

Left: *Chamaecyparis lawsoniana*
Below: *Chamaecyparis obtusa*

Chamaecyparis cone and stem tip

Chamaecyparis
The false cypresses

The false cypress species are large trees, columnar to pyramidal in habit, often growing 100 feet or more in height. They are planted mainly for their lovely foliage, which is scalelike, soft, and rich green to bluish green. *Chamaecyparis* species are often confused with *Thuja* species, the arborvitaes; but their cone structures differ. Each cone scale is attached at its center to a stalk, much like a mushroom. These scales form a round cone usually between ¼ and ⅜ inch long. All the species have attractive grayish or reddish brown bark. The *Chamaecyparis* species are excellent specimen trees. The many cultivars available are used more commonly in contemporary landscapes than the species.

Chamaecyparis species prefer a cool, humid climate and moist, acid, well-drained soil laden with organic matter. However, Atlantic white cedar (*C. thyoides*), native from Maine to Florida, thrives in poorly drained, swampy soils, and cultivars of *C. obtusa* and *C. pisifera* have shown excellent heat tolerance. All tolerate pruning.

Chamaecyparis lawsoniana
Lawson false cypress, Port Orford cedar

Soft scalelike foliage borne in flattened sprays, grayish green to dark green.
Moderate growth rate.
Zones 6 to 8.
40 to 60 feet high, 10 to 20 feet wide.

Lawson false cypress is mainly grown in the West. It grows best where both the soil and the air are moist. Its shredding reddish brown bark adds interest to the landscape. The species can be used as a screen or specimen. 'Allumii' is an attractive columnar form that has rich bluish foliage. The sprays are held vertically and accentuate the rigid formality of this cultivar. 'Fletcheri' is grown for the fluffy, gray green juvenile foliage that often bronzes in winter. It forms a columnar outline. 'Nana' is a globular form that may grow only 6 feet high in 30 years. 'Winston Churchill' is a robust, colorful form with yellow foliage. More than 200 cultivars have been named, and new selections are continuing to appear at a rapid rate.

Chamaecyparis nootkatensis
Nootka or Alaska false cypress

Soft scalelike flattened sprays, grayish green or bluish green on both surfaces, emitting a rather unpleasant odor when bruised.
Moderate growth rate.
Zones 4 to 7 (to 8 on the West Coast).
40 to 50 feet high, 10 to 20 feet wide.

The Nootka false cypress is seldom seen in cultivation, and in most ornamental aspects it is inferior to *C. obtusa* and *C. pisifera*. Its growth habit is conical. The crown is composed of numerous drooping branches with long, pendulous, flattened sprays. It grows best in moist conditions. 'Pendula' is an attractive selection whose branches and sprays hang vertically like curtains, creating a most interesting accent plant.

Chamaecyparis obtusa
Hinoki false cypress

Soft scalelike foliage borne in flattened sprays, shiny dark green above, white X-shaped markings below.
Moderate growth rate.
Zones 4 to 8.

Below: *Chamaecyparis pisifera*
Right: *Cryptomeria japonica*

Height and spread vary widely, depending on cultivar.

Hinoki false cypress forms a tall, slender pyramid with spreading branches and semi-pendulous, frondlike branchlets. The dark green foliage offers excellent color through the seasons, and the shredding reddish brown bark is handsome. This is the most adaptable of the *Chamaecyparis* species. The numerous cultivars enable it to be grown over a wide geographic area. 'Crippsii' forms a broad pyramid, 25 to 30 feet high, with golden yellow new growth that fades with time. The slow-growing 'Nana' has a mounded growth habit and reaches a height of only 2 or 3 feet. Its dark green, almost tufted fronds give its foliage a texture different from that of the species. 'Nana Gracilis' has similar foliage, but it grows larger (6 to 10 feet) and forms a broad pyramid. These cultivars are useful in foundation plantings or rock gardens where foliage texture and slow growth are premium attributes.

Chamaecyparis pisifera
Sawara or Japanese false cypress

Soft scalelike flattened sprays, dark green above, whitish markings below.

Moderate growth rate. Zones 4 to 8.

50 to 70 feet high, 10 to 20 feet wide.

The cultivars, which vary greatly in growth habit and foliage color, are more commonly planted than the species. After *C. obtusa*, this species is the most tolerant of extremes in climate and soil. The reddish brown bark becomes shreddy and is particularly attractive on mature plants.

Cultivars can be broadly categorized into three groups, according to their appearance. One group has soft, feathery foliage with needles that diverge from the stem. Within this group, 'Plumosa' has soft, feathery sprays and an open, airy growth habit. 'Plumosa Aurea' has soft, feathery, golden yellow foliage. Another group has needles closely pressed to long, semi-pendulous branches, creating a stringy appearance. 'Filifera' is a favorite in this group. Its dark green, stringy branches form a loose, broad pyramid 8 to 10 feet high. 'Filifera Aurea' has yellow foliage, and 'Filifera Nana' grows to about 5 feet high. The third group is quite different from the other two. These cultivars have mossy, soft, blue green foliage. 'Squarrosa' forms a broad pyramid of rich bluish foliage; it reaches 25 to 50 feet. 'Squarrosa Pygmaea' is a 3-foot, compact, mounded cultivar with furlike, bluish green foliage. 'Boulevard' ('Cyano-viridis') is a narrow pyramidal form, to 15 feet in height, with bluish green foliage.

Chamaecyparis thyoides
Atlantic white cedar

Scalelike foliage, bluish to grayish green.

Zones 3 to 8.

Moderate growth rate. 40 to 50 feet high, 10 to 20 feet wide.

Although not common in cultivation, this species is an excellent choice for planting along streams, around bogs, in freshwater swamps, and in soggy depressions because it tolerates wet soil. Since the growth habit of this species is slender conical, several plants must be used to achieve an attractive appearance. The handsome bluish green foliage is the richest among the *Chamaecyparis* species.

Cryptomeria japonica
Japanese cryptomeria

Needles ¼ to ¾ inch long, quadrangular in cross section, curving inward toward the stem producing a foxtail appearance, bluish green. Zones 5 to 9.

Below: *Cunninghamia lanceolata*
Right: × *Cupressocyparis leylandii*

*Cryptomeria
cone attachment*

Moderate growth rate.

50 to 60 feet high, 20 to 30 feet wide.

Although this fine evergreen is seldom given its proper due in the United States, it is revered and used in abundance in Japan. Japanese cryptomeria develops a dense, conical to pyramidal outline uniformly covered with branches to the ground. The bluish green needles, which are held 4 to 5 years, become bronzed in cold weather but develop normal coloring with warmer temperatures. Another feature of this tree is the reddish brown bark that peels off in long strips. Older trees that have lost some lower branches are particularly handsome. It can be effectively used as a fast-growing screen, as a background for perennial borders, or in groupings. When planted in sufficient numbers, it provides a splendid grove effect. Rich, deep, light, permeable, acid soil with abundant moisture provides the ideal growing environment. But the species also tolerates hot, dry climates.

'Elegans' and 'Elegans Nana' are compact forms suitable for a small landscape. They have longer needles than the species, which gives them a fluffy look.

*China fir
needle attachment*

Many other forms have been named and are available from specialty conifer growers.

Cunninghamia lanceolata
Common China fir

Needles 1 to 2½ inches long, sharply pointed, arrayed in a flat plane along the stem, dark green, two broad grayish bands on undersurface.

Zones 7 to 9.

Slow, perhaps moderate growth rate under ideal conditions.

40 to 60 feet high, 10 to 20 feet wide.

The China fir (which isn't a true fir) is native to China, where it is planted extensively. It is a pyramidal evergreen with slightly pendulous branches and unusual foliage. However, China fir has such an exotic appearance that it is suitable only as a specimen tree or for novelty use. A major drawback is the retention of dead needles toward the interior of the tree, but not all trees exhibit this trait.

'Glauca' has rich bluish green needles and is especially handsome as a young tree. China fir will grow in most soils but should be protected from drying winds. Overgrown and unsightly specimens can be cut to the ground. Within 3 to 5 years, new growth will reach 8 to 10 feet in height.

× Cupressocyparis leylandii
Leyland cypress

Needles scalelike, soft-textured, bluish green, tightly pressed in bunches along the stem (much like those of arborvitae and false cypress).

Zones 6 to 10.

Fast growth rate.

60 to 70 feet high, 12 to 18 feet wide.

This beautiful evergreen is an intergeneric hybrid between *Chamaecyparis nootkatensis* and *Cupressus macrocarpus*. It was first raised in 1888 in Wales but was not properly classified until 1925. Leyland cypress grows remarkably fast, easily 3 feet per year. Some have grown 60 feet in 20 years.

Left: *Cupressus arizonica*
Below: *Cupressus macrocarpa*

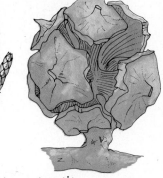

Leyland cypress stem tip

Its growth habit is distinctly columnar to pyramidal, a trait that it maintains into old age. Leyland cypress makes a dense plant without pruning and is ideally suited for screening and windbreaks, especially near the ocean. As a hedge, it has few rivals; some plants have been maintained at 4 feet without adverse effects for more than 20 years. It grows more rapidly in rich soil but easily tolerates adverse soil conditions. Container-grown plants should be chosen for the landscape, since field-grown plants generally do not produce good root systems and are less likely to thrive after transplanting. Its heat tolerance makes it a good choice for southern gardens. 'Castlewellan' has yellow foliage, and 'Silver Dust' has bluish green foliage marked with white variegations. 'Naylor's Blue', which has the bluest foliage color, tends to be the widest spreading and most open in outline.

Cupressus
The cypresses

The *Cupressus* species are the true cypresses, almost all of which are native to dry, warm Mediterranean climates. Most are tender trees and shrubs. They are used mainly on the Pacific Coast and in the Southwest. Their soft, scalelike foliage varies from pale bluish gray to deep green, depending on species and cultivar. Many cypresses have attractive blackish brown or reddish brown bark that is rough or peeling in character.

Cypresses make good hedges, groupings, screens, windbreaks, and accent or specimen plants. Many have a conical or pyramidal growth habit that makes them well suited to formal garden designs. Several cypress species grow in a much more irregular, asymmetrical manner and are best used in contemporary land-scapes. Cypresses need sun, heat, and good drainage, although some will tolerate cooler temperatures and heavier soils.

Cupressus arizonica
Arizona cypress

Foliage scalelike and soft to the touch, light green to bluish green.
Moderate to fast growth rate.
Zones 7 to 9.
30 to 40 feet high, 10 to 15 feet wide.

This softly pyramidal evergreen is seldom cultured north of zone 8, but established specimens can tolerate temperatures of $-5°$ to $-10°$F. Arizona cypress should be used in areas where excessive heat and drought present

Cypress stem tip and cone

cultural problems. It requires well-drained soil and a sunny location. On the East Coast, it does not prove reliable or long-lived. Where adapted, it can be used for screening, grouping, as a specimen, and as a Christmas tree. The reddish brown, varnished-looking bark separates into long, flat strips and adds additional interest. 'Glauca' has blue foliage.

Cupressus macrocarpa
Monterey cypress

Needles scalelike and soft to the touch, medium to dark green.
Zones 7 to 9.
Moderate growth rate.

Left: *Cupressus sempervirens*
Below: *Juniperus chinensis* 'Pfitzerana Glauca'

40 to 50 feet high, 20 to 30 feet wide.

A native of California's Monterey Peninsula, this is the famed cypress that extends its boughs into salt-laden winds from the Pacific Ocean. As a young tree, Monterey cypress is conical, but it becomes more open and wide spreading as it matures. It is effective for hedging and screening. Although Monterey cypress can grow in rocky or sandy soils, it prefers moist, well-drained situations and full sun. It does not do well in areas with hot summers. This cypress is a parent of the Leyland cypress and has imparted its salt tolerance to that species. It is very susceptible to a canker disease.

Cupressus sempervirens
Italian cypress

Needles scalelike and soft to the touch, dark green. Zones 8 to 10 (best in 9 and 10).

Slow to moderate growth rate.

30 to 40 feet high, variable spread.

Italian cypress is quite variable in habit, ranging from a broad, spreading tree with horizontal branches to a type with an upswept outline. The species prefers a dry climate and dry soil and may not survive in poorly drained soils. 'Stricta', the most common columnar form in cultivation, is usually used as a formal accent. In general, it is difficult to blend into a contemporary landscape. The Greeks and Romans regarded its evergreen character as a symbol of immortality.

Several diseases affect Italian cypress. Phomopsis twig blight kills the tips of branches and may progress toward the center of the plant. Cercospora leaf spot is usually manifested by a browning of foliage toward the center of the plant.

Juniperus
The junipers

Junipers are a tolerant and versatile group of plants; their landscape toughness is legendary. In the wild, they grow along the sandy seashore, on windswept mountains, and in the poorest of soils. They are the most widely used evergreen for landscaping, and with proper selection can be grown in all parts of the country. There are no rules of thumb regarding growth habit, foliage, adaptability, or landscape use when describing junipers. Their foliage may be scalelike and soft, prickly as a needle point, or a combination of both. The foliage colors range from yellow, gray, and blue to many shades of green. The cones of junipers are fleshy and appear as small, rounded gray to bluish berries on the branches of female plants. Junipers have the most diverse growth habits of the needle evergreens, ranging from low-growing

ground covers to large trees.

Junipers will grow in any soil that drains well. Full sun is a necessity; junipers become thin and open if grown in deep shade. They are easily transplanted and are most often purchased as container-grown plants.

Junipers are generally healthy, but a few insects and diseases cause problems. Bagworms can defoliate a plant if not stopped in time. Tip moths kill branch tips but seldom cause serious injury. Mites can be a problem, but they are controllable. Juniper twig blight (*Phomopsis juniperovora*) is a serious problem; it kills shoot tips and results in unsightly plants. In the West, junipers commonly suffer from root rot because of overwatering or poor soil drainage. They shouldn't be planted in the same bed with annual flowers or other plants that need frequent watering, especially in heavy soils.

Left: *Juniperus communis* and *Juniperus procumbens*
Below: *Juniperus conferta*

*Juniper with
scalelike leaves*

Juniperus chinensis
Chinese juniper

Needles ⅟₁₆ to ⅓ inch long, vary from green to blue.

Zones 4 to 9.

Slow to moderate growth rate.

Various sizes.

Chinese juniper is represented by many cultivars, ranging from ground covers to medium-sized trees. The plant most often has scalelike and needlelike foliage. One of the most popular forms is 'Gold Coast', which has golden yellow new growth that persists and deepens in color in cold weather. Its habit is gracefully compact and spreading. 'Hetzii' is a vigorous, upright spreading form that may reach 15 feet in height. The rich bluish green, predominantly scalelike foliage and bluish cones are outstanding attributes. 'Kaizuka' ('Torulosa') has the show-stopping name of Hollywood juniper. The vivid green scalelike foliage and twisted growth habit make it unique among Chinese junipers. This cultivar, which reaches approximately 15 to 20 feet in height, doesn't do well in hot, dry climates. 'Keteleeri' is often used in the Midwest for hedging and screening. The medium green scalelike foliage and frosted cones are quite showy. Its outline is broadly pyramidal, and its mature height ranges from 25 to 30 feet. 'Pfitzerana' is the recognized champion of juniper cultivars. The wide-spreading outline, rich green foliage, and inherent garden tough-ness have endeared it to gardeners the world over. The normal landscape height ranges between 5 and 10 feet; its spread is about twice its height. It has produced many forms over the years including 'Pfitzerana Aurea', with gold-blushed new growth; 'Compacta', a bushy compact form growing ultimately 2 to 3 feet high and 6 to 8 feet wide; and 'Glauca', with bluish green summer foliage, becoming purplish blue in winter. 'Robusta Green' is an upright form, 15 feet in height, with tufted, brilliant green, mostly scalelike foliage. 'San Jose' is a ground-cover form that grows 1 to 1½ feet high and 6 to 8 feet wide. The sage green foliage is composed of both scale-like and needlelike leaves. The variety *sargentii* rates as one of the best ground-cover junipers. The rich bluish green needles are borne on a framework 1½ to 2 feet high and 7½ to 9 feet wide. It is tolerant of dry soil and salt. In addition, there are many other cultivars of Chinese juniper, some only regionally adapted. It is always wise to ask at your local nursery about the best cultivars for the area. For example, 'San Jose' may contract juniper blight under midwestern (zone 5) conditions; but in the South (zone 8), it has proven reliable and blight-free.

Juniperus communis
Common juniper

Foliage sharply needlelike, ½ to ⅝ inch long, usually with a broad white band on the upper surface; bluish green needles occur in 3s around the stem.

Zones 2 to 6 (to 8 on the West Coast).

Slow to moderate growth rate.

Varies in size from low, spreading shrubs to upright trees.

The common juniper makes its home in the most inhospitable climates and soils. Rocks, trampled pastures, and mountainsides provide the ideal environment for this widespread species. It is more shade-tolerant than other junipers. The species is not common in American landscapes but is used in Europe. The cultivars include 'Compressa', a dense, cone-shaped form; *J.c.* var. *depressa,* a spreading shrub rarely more than 4 feet high; 'Depressa

Below: *Juniperus horizontalis*
Right: *Juniperus scopulorum*

Aurea', with yellow foliage; 'Gold Beach', 4 to 6 inches high, mat-forming, with yellow new growth that later turns green; 'Hibernica' (Irish) and 'Suecica' (Swedish), upright forms with bluish green needlelike foliage. In general, the *J. communis* types are not preferable to *J. chinensis* or *J. horizontalis* except in extremely cold climates and impossible soils.

Juniper with needlelike leaves

Juniperus conferta
Shore juniper

Foliage sharply needlelike, ½ to ¾ inch long, borne in 3s, rich green to bluish green, with a whitish band above.

Zones 6 to 9.

Moderate growth rate.

1 to 1½ feet high, 6 to 9 feet wide.

There is no low-growing juniper that can compete with shore juniper as a fast-growing ground cover. Given proper drainage, it will succeed in sand, loam, or clay. The rich green carpet sparkles on a sunny day. Unfortunately, it does not have good cold tolerance and stems die back when temperatures drop below −10°F. In winter it tends to become yellowish green, but quickly returns to rich green with the onset of warm weather. 'Blue Pacific' grows about 9 to 12 inches high and has rich ocean blue–green foliage. 'Emerald Sea' is similar to 'Blue Pacific', but its foliage is greener. Both are excellent cultivars.

Juniperus horizontalis
Creeping juniper

Needles primarily scalelike; soft to the touch; bluish green, turning shades of plum purple in winter.

Zones 3 to 9.

Slow to moderate growth rate.

1 to 2 feet high, 4 to 8 feet wide.

Many gardeners consider the creeping juniper species and cultivars to be the aristocrats of ground-cover junipers. Most important is their wide geographic adaptability and the great number of cultivars (approximately 50) that are available. Their ability to cover broad expanses of bare ground is well known. All are adaptable to extremes of soil and climatic conditions. The more common selections include 'Bar Harbor', 8 to 12 inches high, 8 to 10 feet wide, with rich bluish foliage, forming dense cover; 'Douglasii' ('Waukegan'), an old but popular form, 1 to 1½ feet high, 6 to 9 feet wide, steel-blue foliage turning grayish purple in winter; 'Plumosa', wide-spreading dense form, 2 feet high, 10 feet wide, rich gray-green, purplish in winter; 'Wiltoni' ('Blue Rug', 'Blue Carpet'), a flat-growing form, 4 to 6 inches high, 6 to 8 feet wide, intense blue foliage assumes a slight purple tinge in winter, females produce

good quantities of grayish cones. Creeping juniper is susceptible to juniper blight; one of the most popular cultivars, 'Plumosa' ('Andorra'), is the most susceptible.

Juniperus procumbens
Japanese garden juniper

Sharply pointed needles, ⅓ inch, rich bluish green.

Zones 4 to 9.

Slow growth rate.

1 to 2 feet high, 10 to 15 feet wide.

Few ground-cover junipers can equal a well-grown specimen of the Japanese garden juniper. The rich bluish green needle color holds throughout the seasons. 'Nana' is more compact than the species, not so much in ultimate size but in the tightly knit branching pattern and needle density that results in a solid cover. 'Variegata' is a bluish green form that is splashed with creamy white markings. In warm, moist weather, juniper blight can be a problem.

Below: *Juniperus squamata*
Right: *Juniperus virginiana*

Juniperus sabina
Savin juniper

Needles primarily scalelike and soft to the touch, potent odor when bruised, often sage green.

Zones 3 to 7 (to 8 on the West Coast).

Slow growth rate.

Varies from spreading ground covers to large upright shrubs.

Savin juniper cultivars (rather than the species) are most commonly planted in the United States. They include 'Arcadia', with scalelike, grass-green, blight-resistant foliage, 1 foot high, 4 feet wide; 'Broadmoor', a dwarf, low-spreading form, 12 to 18 inches high, 2 to 4 feet wide, with soft grayish green foliage and resistance to juniper blight; 'Skandia', similar to 'Arcadia', with pale grayish green, needlelike foliage, 1 to 1½ feet high, 10 feet wide; variety *tamariscifolia* (familiarly known as Tam juniper), a low-spreading, mounded form with bluish green foliage, 18 inches high and 10 to 15 feet across.

Juniperus scopulorum
Rocky Mountain juniper

Needles scalelike, soft-textured, light green to rich blue.

Zones 3 to 7 (to 9 on the West Coast).

Slow growth rate.

30 to 40 feet high, 15 feet wide.

Juniperus scopulorum is closely akin to *J. virginiana*. It appears to be best adapted to a dry climate and is widely used in the Plains and Rocky Mountain states. Unfortunately, it is not well adapted to eastern conditions; it may contract severe cedar apple rust and blight and become unsightly. Some of the richest blue-foliage forms of juniper have been selected from this species, including 'Blue Heaven', 'Medora', 'Pathfinder', 'Welchii', and 'Wichita Blue'. A novelty is 'Skyrocket', with bluish green foliage and a "rocket" outline. 'Tolleson's Weeping' has silvery blue foliage and stringlike arching branches. There is also a green-foliage form of 'Tolleson's Weeping'. It is an excellent choice for specimen use, hedging, and screening.

Juniperus squamata
Singleseed juniper

Needles sharply pointed, silvery blue-green.

Zones 4 to 8.

Slow growth rate.

Size varies, depending on cultivar.

The species is not commonly cultivated in the United States. 'Meyeri', with striking silvery blue needles, is the most commonly planted cultivar. It grows 6 to 8 feet high, 4 to 6 feet wide, and is an upright shrub with "fishtail" leaders. Unfortunately, dead needles persist, resulting in an unsightly plant. 'Blue Star' is a branch sport of 'Meyeri'. Its foliage is the same rich color, but it is is rounded, squat, 2 to 2½ feet high, 4 to 6 feet across. 'Prostrata' has light bluish green needles that may turn slightly brownish or pinkish at the tips in winter; it grows 12 inches high and is broad-spreading. All cultivars display excellent resistance to blight as well as adaptability to extremes of soil and climate. They are somewhat difficult to use in conventional landscaping because of their strong coloration. In a rock or specialty garden their bright colors can be put to effective use because they draw visual attention to otherwise uninteresting areas.

Juniperus virginiana
Eastern red cedar

Either scalelike or needlelike leaves arranged in opposite pairs along the stem, deep green becoming yellow or brownish green in winter.

Zones 3 to 9.

Medium growth rate.

Grows 40 to 50 feet high and 10 to 20 feet wide; variable in habit over its native range.

Cursed by many, acclaimed by few, eastern red cedar is among the most adaptable of all evergreen species. The

Left: *Larix decidua*   Bottom: *Larix* cone

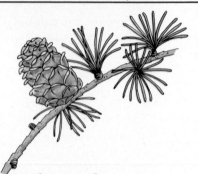

species will grow in pure sand or clay and can withstand drought, saline conditions, and the vagaries of weather. In winter the foliage often discolors to a dirty green. The most popular cultivars include 'Burkii', with needles and some scalelike foliage, bluish green turning steel blue with a slight purplish cast in winter, 10 to 25 feet high; and 'Canaertii', a popular tree form, 30 to 35 feet, with rich dark green, tufted, scalelike foliage and an attractive open branching habit. 'Gray Owl' is similar to 'Pfitzerana' but is smaller and has soft, silvery gray foliage. 'Silver Spreader' is similar to 'Gray Owl' but with more silvery foliage. Eastern red cedar is quite susceptible to cedar apple rust; the large tumorlike growths are unattractive but are not very harmful to the plant. However, when apples or hawthorns are growing nearby, this species and *J. scopulorum* should not be planted, or the growths should be removed and destroyed.

Larix
The larches

Larches are deciduous conifers. They have rich green, angular needles that turn golden to brownish yellow in fall. In the landscape, they are best reserved for groves and mass plantings. Although most larches prefer moist, well-drained soil, our native tamarack (*L. laricina*) grows in bogs. The larches are not well suited to hot, dry conditions and do not grow in zones 8 to 10.

Larix decidua
European or common larch

Needles 1 to 1½ inches long, rich green, turning ochre yellow before dropping in fall, are borne singly on long shoots or 30 to 40 together from short spurs on older branches.

Zones 2 to 6.
Moderate to fast growth rate.
70 to 75 feet high, 25 to 30 feet wide.
The European larch is the most common species in cultivation. Its outline is softly pyramidal, and in youth it has a supple appearance. This species does not grow old gracefully; it tends to hold dead branches and old cones. The young cones are often a rich reddish purple and look like small ornaments in early spring. The species has adapted to a variety of soil conditions, but it is not tolerant to heat and seldom performs well south of zone 6. Larch case-bearer can be a serious pest; it eats the interior of the needle, leaving nothing but a brown outer casing. Larches are particularly attractive in groves along streams or on hillsides. 'Pendula', a weeping form with extremely pendulous branchlets, makes a strong accent plant.

Larch cone and needle spurs

Larix kaempferi
Japanese larch

Needles 1 to 1½ inches long, rich green changing to golden yellow before dropping in fall, are borne in manner similar to that of *L. decidua*.
Zones 4 to 7.
Moderate to fast growth rate.
70 to 90 feet high, 25 to 40 feet wide.
A beautiful conifer, usually pyramidal in outline but gracefully open, with slender pendulous branchlets. The most ornamental of the larches, it is ideally suited to parks, golf courses, and spacious estates. A hillside covered with Japanese larch,

Left: *Metasequoia glyptostroboides*
Below: *Picea abies*

especially in fall, is spectacular. There is a weeping form similar to *L. decidua* 'Pendula'.

Larix laricina
Tamarack, American larch

Needles 1 inch long bright bluish green, turning rich yellow in fall, drop in fall.

Zones 1 to 4 or 5.

Slow to moderate growth rate.

30 to 50 feet high, 10 to 15 feet wide.

This is one of the most beautiful species, especially in its rich golden fall color. Its tolerance to wet soils is legendary, and in fact it tends to resent cultivation. The cones are the smallest of the larch species, and it has a more narrow growth habit than the other species. For naturalizing in cold climates and wet soils, it is a good choice.

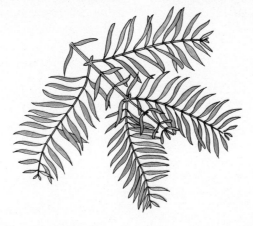

Metasequoia branchlets

Metasequoia glyptostroboides
Dawn redwood

Needles are a rich green, ½ inch long, turning tan to orangish brown before dropping in the fall. They are borne in a flat plane on branchlets that also drop in fall.

Zones 5 to 8.

Fast growth rate.

75 to 100 feet high, 25 feet wide.

This deciduous conifer is a relic that was "rediscovered" in the wild in Szechwan province, China, in 1944. Since then the species has been widely planted. Specimens over 100 feet high have been recorded. It has a feathery growth habit; in winter, its habit offers a silhouette of uniformly spaced branches. The shreddy, reddish brown bark and buttressed trunk provide winter interest. For maximum growth, plant dawn redwood in rich, moist, acid, well-drained soil. It is excellent as a quick screen, in a mass planting, or as a large specimen tree. A canker has been reported and in some areas has proven troublesome.

Picea
The spruces

Spruces, like firs, are cold-climate species and do not perform well in the heat of the South (zone 8 and higher). As a group, they are more tolerant of unfavorable soil and environmental conditions than firs, and some species are found native on infertile, dry soils. They are tall, symmetrical, conical trees. Many cultivars spread and weep. The dark green needles are usually quadrangular in cross section, which separates them from the flat-needled firs. The male and female cones are borne on separate parts of the same tree: male on lower branches, female on upper. At maturity, the cones hang down; they may persist for a year or more.

Spruces make excellent specimen plants, groupings, and screens.

Left: *Picea brewerana*   Below: *Picea glauca*

Their symmetrical, vertical habit is most effective in a large-scale, formal landscape. Spruces grow best in a sunny location in moderately moist, well-drained soil. They are most easily transplanted in the spring. Spruces are susceptible to few serious diseases or insects, but canker, gall-forming aphids, mites, and bagworms can be troublesome.

Picea abies
Norway spruce

Needles ½ to 1 inch long, stiff, angular in cross section, dark green.
Zones 3 to 8.
Moderate growth rate.
40 to 60 feet high, 25 to 30 feet wide.

The most commonly used landscape spruce in the northern states, Norway spruce forms a stiff pyramid in youth but loosens with age and becomes rather graceful. As a specimen it has merit, though it tends to dominate a landscape. Its most effective use is for windbreaks, screens, mass plantings, or groupings. This species has more than 135 cultivars. 'Clanbrasiliana', discovered in 1836, grows in a low, dense, flat-topped mound 3 to 4 feet high, usually wider than its height. 'Nidiformis' (bird's nest spruce) superficially resembles a nest because its somewhat flat top has a depression in the middle; its dense growth may reach 3 to 6 feet in height after many years. 'Pendula' and 'Inversa' are only two of the many weeping types. 'Repens' is a handsome, wide-spreading form that slowly builds up in the center to form a uniform cushionlike mass. All these cultivars are ideal accent plants.

Spruce cone

Picea brewerana
Brewer's spruce

Needles ½ to 1 inch long, either flattened or somewhat triangular in cross section, lustrous dark bluish green.
Zones 5 to 7.
Moderate growth rate.
40 to 60 feet high, 20 feet wide.

Not a commonly planted spruce, *P. brewerana* has a graceful, almost pendulous branching habit. The strong central leader supports secondary branches of a horizontal or slightly pendulous nature. From these, tertiary branchlets hang like curtains. As a specimen or accent plant, it has few rivals. It grows best in a cool, moist climate.

Picea glauca
White spruce

Needles ½ to ¾ inch long, quadrangular in cross section, pale or grayish green, with a strange odor when bruised.

Zones 2 to 6 (to 8 on the West Coast).
Slow to moderate growth rate.
40 to 60 feet high, 10 to 20 feet wide.

The species is seldom used in modern landscapes, although it is tolerant of drought and cold. The needle color is not particularly rich, and it suffers in comparison with the rich blue and dark green spruces. *P. g.* 'Conica', dwarf white or Alberta spruce, produces broad, dense cones and light green, densely set needles that radiate around the stem. It grows slowly (2 to 4 inches per year) and attains a height of 10 to 12 feet only after a period of 25 to 30 years. Dwarf white spruce is very common in commerce. *P. g.* 'Densata' is a slow-growing, conical form 20 to 40 feet high, with densely set needles. White spruce and its cultivars can be effectively used in the Plains and western states where dry soils prevail. Mites can be a problem.

Below: *Picea mariana* 'Nana'
Right: *Picea pungens* 'Glauca'

Picea mariana
Black spruce

Needles ¼ to ½ inch long, angular in cross section, dark bluish green.

Zones 2 to 5 (to 6 on the West Coast).

Slow growth rate.

30 to 40 feet high, 10 to 15 feet wide.

The black spruce is a cold-climate species and should be used only in the recommended zones. In hot, dry climates, it becomes thin, open, and ragged. In Maine, it grows at the edges of cold sphagnum bogs, where it forms a narrow, spirelike tree. Several cultivars are more widely adapted. 'Doumetii' is a slow-growing, densely pyramidal form with rich bluish green needles. 'Nana' is a compact, mounded shrub with dark bluish green needles. Both work well in rockeries or mixed borders.

Picea omorika
Serbian spruce

Needles ½ to 1 inch long, different from most spruces because needles are flat and marked with two white lines above, lustrous dark green below.

Zones 4 to 7 (to 8 on the West Coast).

Slow growth rate.

50 to 60 feet high, 20 to 25 feet wide.

This tree has a remarkably slender trunk and short ascending or drooping branches forming a very narrow, pyramidal shape. It is a one-of-a-kind evergreen that deserves greater use. The dark green needles are as rich as those of any other evergreen. Its distinctive growth habit makes it useful as a specimen, in groupings, or for a formal accent. This spruce is fairly tolerant of urban environments and will grow in limestone as well as acid soils. It is susceptible to windburn in extremely cold winters and does not tolerate the extreme heat of the South. This slow-growing tree takes 50 to 60 years to attain its mature height.

Picea orientalis
Oriental spruce

Needles ¼ to ½ inch long (the shortest of the cultivated spruces), densely set along the branches, lustrous dark green.

Zones 4 to 7 (to 8 on the West Coast).

Slow growth rate.

50 to 60 feet high, 10 to 15 feet wide.

Along with *P. omorika*, *P. orientalis* is considered one of the aristocrats of the spruces. It forms a dense, narrow pyramid of lustrous, dark green needles. The new cones are a rich reddish purple and look like small strawberries over the tree canopy. It tolerates infertile, gravelly soils and urban conditions. Because of its attractive habit, specimen use is warranted. It is particularly effective in groupings. 'Gowdy' is a narrow, columnar, slow-growing form. 'Pendula' ('Weeping Dwarf') is a compact, slow-growing form that has pendulous branchlets.

Picea pungens 'Glauca'
Colorado blue spruce

Needles ¾ to 1¼ inches long, stiff and sharp-pointed, bluish green to blue, radiating around stem to form a brushlike mass.

Zones 3 to 7.

30 to 60 feet high, 10 to 20 feet wide.

From the Midwest to the Pacific Coast, blue spruces punctuate landscape horizons. The narrow to broad pyramidal outline with horizontal stiff branches graces many homes. The tree is beautiful when used in groups in spacious lawns, but it is obtrusive at the corner of a house or in front of a picture window. Because needle color varies so much, purchase named cultivars to ensure that the foliage will be blue. This variety displays excellent soil and climatic tolerances.

Left: *Pinus aristata* Below: *Pinus bungeana*

'Hoopsii', 'Moerheimii', 'Pendens' ('Koster'), and 'Thompsonii' have silvery blue needles. 'Glauca Pendula' is a pendulous, blue-needled form that crawls and sprawls, and 'Montgomery' forms a compact shrub with silvery blue needles. All of these are commercially available. Cooley spruce gall aphids and tussock moths are problems on this tree.

Pinus
The pines

The pines offer the greatest diversity of habit and adaptability of all the needle evergreens and are the largest group of conifers, with 90 or so species. On this continent, there is no place in the United States or Canada where pines cannot be grown. Pines such as *P. ponderosa, P. taeda,* and *P. strobus* are major sources of lumber.

Pines are generally large trees, often pyramidal or conical in youth, and more open and irregular with age. Most species are categorized and identified by the number of needles contained in each bundle, ranging from 1 to 5. In general, the 2-needle pines are more tolerant of adverse growing conditions than the 3- and 5-needle types. Pines bear male and female cones on the same tree. The cones may fall the first season after maturing or persist for many years.

In landscaping, pines have been used for every conceivable purpose, including specimens, screens, windbreaks, topiary, hedges, and even ground covers. Their growth habits vary widely, depending upon the species, and in some cases change dramatically throughout the life of a particular species. Usually, a good selection of pine species and cultivars is available and suitable for any landscape use. Many pines have unusually colored or textured bark. The beautiful orange to reddish brown bark of Scotch pine (*P. sylvestris*) and Japanese red pine (*P. densiflora*), the sycamorelike bark of lacebark pine (*P. bungeana*), and the white, gray, and brown bark of Austrian pine create additional interest in the landscape.

Pines are more tolerant of adverse soil and climatic conditions than firs and spruces. They require full sun for maximum growth but will tolerate shade. Pines withstand pruning; removing half of the new candle growth (when new needles are one-half to three-quarters of their full length) causes new buds to form below the cut. Young pines (2 to 5 years old) are often purchased as container-grown plants and may be planted any time. Pines of all ages are most successfully moved or transplanted in the spring. Pines are not free of problems; rusts, cankers, scales, and shoot moths can be particularly troublesome.

Ponderosa pine needle and cone attachment

Right: *Pinus cembra*
Below left: *Pinus bungeana* **needles**
Below right: *Pinus bungeana* **bark**

Pinus aristata
Bristlecone pine

Needles in 5s, 1 to 1¾ inches long, persisting 14 to 17 years, dark green and often covered with whitish resin drops that superficially resemble scale insects.

Zones 4 to 7 (to 9 on the West Coast).

Slow growth rate.

10 to 20 feet high, variable spread.

The bristlecone pine is considered to be the oldest living tree on earth, with some specimens surpassing 4,000 years. The growth habit is decidedly unusual, seldom adhering to any written description. It may be single- or multiple-trunked, flat-topped, or broad-spreading, but it is always irregular. The slow growth allows it to be kept in scale with the contemporary landscape. As an accent plant, it has little competition and can be integrated very effectively with dwarf conifers, rhododendrons, heathers, and dwarf spireas. It tolerates a wide range of soils and climates.

Pinus banksiana
Jack pine

Needles in 2s, 1 to 2 inches long, persisting 2 to 4 years, light to dull green, often yellowish green in winter.

Zones 2 to 7.

Slow to moderate growth rate.

35 to 50 feet high, 20 to 30 feet wide.

The Jack pine has that rare ability to grow where even the most noxious weeds fear to tread. Few Jack pines make outstanding specimens because their habit is rather open and wide spreading. The cones may persist for many years; this gradual accumulation can give the plant a messy appearance. For use in sand or clay soils, it has few rivals. It is frequently used in windbreaks, shelterbelts, and mass plantings.

Pinus bungeana
Lacebark pine

Needles in 3s, 2 to 4 inches long, stiff and sharply pointed, persisting 3 to 4 years, lustrous dark green.

Zones 4 to 8.

Slow growth rate.

30 to 50 feet high, 20 to 35 feet wide.

Lacebark pine is pyramidal to rounded in youth, often with many trunks, and becomes more open and irregular with age. The bark peels off in patches, exposing areas of gray, grayish green, and brown. This species tolerates acid, limestone, and relatively dry soils. For maximum effect, the lower branches should be removed to expose and showcase the handsome bark. It is an excellent specimen plant whose use is limited only by the imagination of the gardener.

Pinus canariensis
Canary Island pine

Needles in 3s, 9 to 12 inches long, glossy green.

Zones 8 to 10.

Fast growth rate.

60 to 100 feet high, narrower spread.

As a young tree, Canary Island pine is pyramidal in shape; with age, it develops a tiered appearance, and eventually it matures into a stately tree with a rounded crown. The long droopy needles give the tree a soft quality. These tender pines prefer hot, dry conditions. They make good windbreaks and screens, and are often planted in groups. Because they grow quickly to a large size, Canary Island pines are best suited for open and expansive settings. They are unusual among pines in being able to sprout new shoots from cut stumps and branch stubs.

Pinus cembra
Swiss stone pine

Needles in 5s, 2 to 3 inches (sometimes to 5 inches) long, persisting 4 to 5 years, dark green on the outside, bluish white bands inside.

Zones 4 to 7 (to 8 on the West Coast).

Slow growth rate.

30 to 40 feet high, narrow spread.

Left: *Pinus contorta*
Below: *Pinus densiflora 'Oculus-draconis'* needles

This is a stately evergreen, usually densely columnar to pyramidal in youth, becoming more open with age. Its primary use is as a specimen or in groupings of 3 to 5 where a bold element is required. Swiss stone pine thrives in moist, acid, well-drained soil.

Pinus cembroides
Pinyon pine

Needles usually in 3s, sometimes 2s, 1 to 2 inches long, dark green.
Zones 5 to 7 (to 8 on the West Coast).
Slow growth rate.
15 to 20 feet high.

The pinyon pine is a rather bushy, small tree and is often grown as a shrub. The species *P. edulis* is similar to pinyon pine, except its needles are chiefly in 2s. Both are used in the Plains and Rocky Mountain states where dry soil tolerance is essential. They are most effective when planted in groups.

Pinus contorta
Shore pine

Needles in 2s, 1½ to 2 inches long, dark green and twisted.
Zones 5 to 7 (to 8 on the West Coast).
Slow to medium growth rate.
20 to 30 feet high, 10 to 12 feet wide.

The shore pine, with its irregular growth habit, is widely used in landscapes in the Pacific Northwest. One variety, the lodgepole pine (*P. contorta* var. *latifolia*), is straight and untwisted, and is used away from the coast. Lodgepole pine thrives in several areas of the Midwest but suffers by comparison with white pine and other more ornamental species.

Pinus densiflora
Japanese red pine

Needles in 2s, 3 to 5 inches long, lustrous bright green, persisting 3 years.
Zones 4 to 7 (to 8 on the West Coast).
Medium growth rate.
40 to 60 feet high, similar spread.

This is a splendid pine with rich foliage, attractive bark, and a unique growth habit. The needles appear to be tufted and perched like butterflies on the upper sides of the branches. The bark on older branches becomes orangish to reddish brown and peels off in thin scales. The trunks frequently grow in a crooked or leaning manner, the branches spread horizontally, and the crown develops into a rather broad and flat shape. It adds an artistic touch to the landscape when used as a specimen or in loose groupings. The orangish to reddish bark brightens the winter landscape, especially in northern areas where drab grays and browns predominate. It has no special soil requirements other than good drainage. Some interesting cultivars include 'Oculus-draconis' (dragon's-eye pine), whose needles are marked with alternating yellow and green bands, and 'Pendula', a weeping form with rich green needles that may be used as a ground cover. 'Pendula' is effective

when allowed to drape over rock walls and raised planters. 'Umbraculifera' (Tanyosho pine) is a beautiful, many-stemmed, upright spreading form that terminates in an umbrellalike head. The branches develop the excellent orange-red bark of the species. It usually grows 8 to 10 feet high, but 40-year-old plants may be 25 feet high. There is a compact form that grows about one-half the size of 'Umbraculifera'.

Pinus flexilis
Limber pine

Needles in 5s, 2½ to 3½ inches long, slightly twisted, dark green to bluish green, persisting 5 to 6 years.
Zones 4 to 7.
Slow growth rate.
30 to 50 feet high, 15 to 35 feet wide.

This beautiful pine has a soft texture and rich, dark bluish green needles. In youth, the habit is a broad pyramid that opens with age. Limber pine makes a lovely specimen. It is

Left: *Pinus flexilis* Below: *Pinus mugo* var. *mugo*

extremely adaptable and has proven to be one of the best in the difficult western and midwestern climates. Two cultivars of note are 'Glauca', with rich bluish green needles, and 'Glauca Pendula', with rich bluish green needles and a wide-spreading growth habit.

Pinus koraiensis
Korean pine

Needles in 5s, 3½ to 4½ inches long, overall gray to bluish green color, persisting 3 years.

Zones 4 to 7 (to 8 on the West Coast).

30 to 40 feet high, 10 to 15 feet wide.

In several respects, Korean pine is similar to *P. flexilis*, *P. peuce*, and *P. strobus*. It has excellent bluish green needle color and cold tolerance. Its loosely pyramidal growth habit makes it ideal for informal screening or grouping. It grows in any well-drained soil.

Pinus mugo
Mugo pine

Needles in 2s, 1 to 2 inches (sometimes as long as 3 inches) long, medium to dark green, persisting 5 or more years.

Zones 2 to 7 (to 8 on the West Coast).

Slow growth rate.

Height is quite variable, from 3 feet to 40 or 50 feet.

Mugo pine presents a dilemma to gardeners because the cute, diminutive cushion that the nursery salesperson says grows only 3 feet high may end up 10 feet, 20 feet, or taller. There is no accurate way to gauge their ultimate size except to purchase plants that are still less than 3 feet after 5 to 10 years in the growing field. Inspect nursery plants to see how much pruning has been done to keep them small. Mugo pine is perfect for use as a foundation plant, in groupings, or in a low, billowy unpruned hedge. Although most of these plants in nurseries are low, broad-spreading, and bushy, some as large as 35 to 45 feet are known.

Mugo pine is an excellent choice for alkaline as well as acid soils. Varieties *mugo* and *pumilo* are relatively low-growing forms. Many named cultivars exist, some of which are reliably low-growing, but they are difficult to find commercially. Scale is occasionally a problem for these pines.

Pinus nigra
Austrian pine

Needles in 2s, 4 to 6 inches long, stiff and sharply pointed, dark green, persisting 4 years.

Zones 4 to 7 (to 8 on the West Coast).

35 to 50 feet high, 15 to 25 feet wide.

The Austrian pine was at one time a choice evergreen for screens, windbreaks, and specimen use in the East and Midwest. In recent years, however, Diplodia tip blight and pine nematodes have resulted in branch dieback, and entire trees have been killed in eastern states. The outline is broadly pyramidal in youth, becoming more open and

irregular with age. The bark develops wide, flat areas that are mottled with gray, white, and brown. The effect is particularly striking in the winter landscape. Austrian pine is a favored tree because it displays excellent tolerance to drought, salt, urban conditions, sand, clay, acidity, and alkalinity. It will continue to be used in landscapes, but you should consider its pest problems before investing in large plantings. Several varieties may prove more resistant than the species, but they need additional testing.

Pinus parviflora
Japanese white pine

Needles in 5s, forming brushlike tufts at the ends of the branches, persisting 3 to 4 years, bluish green.

Zones 4 to 7 (to 8 on the West Coast).

Slow growth rate.

25 to 50 feet high, variable spread.

Japanese white pine is not common in American landscapes but deserves consideration. It has

Below: *Pinus nigra* bark   **Right:** *Pinus peuce*

striking bluish green needles (especially on 'Glauca'), a wide-spreading, rather unusual growth habit, and lustrous, waxy, thick-scaled cones that mature from greenish to rich brown. Japanese white pine is an excellent specimen tree, which with age becomes even more striking because of its irregular, wide-spreading branches. It is tolerant of varied soils, including salty soils, but requires excellent drainage.

Pinus peuce
Balkan, Macedonian pine

Needles in 5s, 3 to 4 inches long, dark green, persisting 3 years.

Zones 4 to 7.

Slow growth rate.

30 to 60 feet high, narrow spread.

Pinus peuce mirrors the form and general characteristics of *P. cembra*, but it is slightly faster growing. It maintains its dense, columnar to pyramidal habit into old age,

making it a choice tree for screens. It displays excellent adaptability to diverse soils as long as they are moist and well drained.

Pinus ponderosa
Western yellow pine

Needles in 3s or sometimes 2s, 5 to 10 inches long, yellowish to dark green, persisting 3 years.

Zones 3 to 6 (to 8 on the West Coast).

Moderate growth rate.

60 to 100 feet high under cultivation, 25 to 30 feet wide.

Pinus ponderosa is an important timber species in western North America. In youth it is narrow and pyramidal in shape, becoming irregularly cylindrical with age. It is a large tree, with attractive orange bark, but in most landscapes it soon grows out of scale. 'Glauca' has attractive bluish green needles.

Pinus pumila
Japanese stone pine, dwarf Siberian pine

Needles in 5s, 1½ to 3 inches long, rich bluish green, persisting 4 to 5 years.

Zones 5 to 7.

Slow growth rate.

Height is quite variable, from 1 or 2 feet to 8 or 10 feet, wide spread.

This is a magnificent landscape species that is finally attracting the attention of gardeners and nursery owners. The dwarf, bushy, spreading habit provides an alternative to the many large, massive pine species. For use in foundations, borders, unpruned hedges, and groupings, this plant has no rivals among the pines. It displays wide soil tolerance—particularly to rocky, gravelly, and sandy soils—but it grows best in moist, well-drained soils. Most plants are seed-grown. They vary greatly in growth habit, from prostrate ground covers to upright 8-foot-high shrubs.

Pinus resinosa
Red pine

Needles in 2s, 5 to 6 inches long, medium to dark green, persisting 4 years.

Zones 2 to 6 (to 7 on the West Coast), best in a cold climate.

Moderate growth rate.

50 to 80 feet high, variable spread.

The red pine is seldom employed for landscaping outside its native range. It is broadly pyramidal, but its desirable ornamental characteristics are minimal compared with those of other species. Its reddish brown bark is superficially scaly and provides seasonal interest. The red pine tolerates exposed, dry, acid, sandy, and gravelly soils. It is considered second only to *P. banksiana* in its ability to grow in such situations.

Pinus rigida
Pitch pine

Needles in 3s, 3 to 4½ inches long, stiff and sharply pointed, dark green, persisting 2 or 3 years.

Below: *Pinus strobus*   **Right:** *Pinus sylvestris*

Zones 4 to 7.

Moderate growth rate.

40 to 60 feet high, 30 to 50 feet wide .

Pitch pine is seldom given credit for anything except growing where few other plants can survive. As a colonizer of infertile, sandy, or clay soils, it has few peers. In the native environment it assumes many shapes, usually compact and gnarled, but it can be a rather handsome tree if provided with reasonably good soil and adequate moisture. Its principal landscape uses are in irregular masses, screens, and groupings. It displays excellent salt tolerance and can be used in coastal areas where other pines falter.

Pinus strobus
Eastern white pine

Needles in 5s, 3 to 5 inches long, soft texture, rich green to bluish green, persisting 2 to 3 years.

Zones 3 to 8.

Moderate to fast growth rate.

50 to 80 feet high, 20 to 40 feet wide.

White pine has a graceful, dignified appearance. In youth it forms a pyramid of soft almost furry foliage. With age, the crown becomes open, the branches grow almost horizontally, and the needles are borne in a graceful, plumelike manner. Many of the older needles drop in the fall or when the plant is stressed. White pine is a superior specimen tree but can also be used for screens, hedges, and groupings. It is tolerant of many kinds of soil and performs well in the East, the Midwest, and the upper South. Many cultivars have been named. 'Fastigiata' is a narrow columnar form in youth, becoming wider with age, with branches arising at a 45° angle. 'Glauca' has bluish green needles. 'Nana' is a broad, pyramidal to rounded, dense bush. 'Pendula' is a weeping type with long branches that sweep the ground. Occasionally, plants in the Midwest and West develop chlorosis because of alkaline soils. White

pine blister rust and white pine weevil can be troublesome.

Pinus sylvestris
Scotch pine

Needles in 2s, 1 to 4 inches long, twisted, bluish green, persisting 3 years.

Zones 2 to 8.

Moderate growth rate.

30 to 60 feet high, 30 to 40 feet wide.

Scotch pine is the most common Christmas tree in midwestern and northern markets. But it also has much to offer as a landscape plant. The rich bluish needles provide a contrast to the typical "sea" of green produced by most pines. Irregularly pyramidal in youth, it eventually becomes open and wide spreading, with a flat or round top approaching an umbrella shape. The orangish to brown bark peels off in papery flakes. This is one of the easiest pines to transplant and is adaptable to a variety of

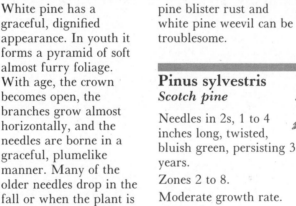

White pine needle and cone attachment

soils. For groupings, informal screens, or as an accent plant, it is a solid choice. Two common cultivars are 'Fastigiata', with a columnar habit, and 'Watereri', a beautiful, rich bluish green, with a densely pyramidal to flat-topped form and the orangish brown bark of the species.

Pinus thunbergiana
Japanese black pine

Needles in 2s, 2½ to 7 inches long, stiff and sharply pointed (similar to *P. nigra*), lustrous dark green, persisting 3 to 5 years.

Zones 5 to 7 (to 9 on the West Coast).

Moderate growth rate.

20 to 40 feet high, variable spread.

The Japanese black pine makes an elegant, artistic addition to any garden. Its habit is broadly pyramidal, but the branches may dip, dive, spread, and turn. It is frequently ungainly in youth. The species shows excellent salt tolerance and is an ideal choice for sandy soils along coastal areas. It is not particularly cold-hardy, and severe needle browning may occur when temperatures drop below −10°F. It is more heat-tolerant than might be expected. Occasionally, shoot tip borers can cause problems.

Pinus virginiana
Virginia pine, scrub pine

Needles in 2s, 1½ to 3 inches long, somewhat twisted, yellow green to dark green, may turn yellow green in winter, persisting 3 to 4 years.

Zones 4 to 8.

Slow to moderate growth rate.

15 to 40 feet high, 10 to 30 feet wide.

Pinus virginiana is an open, broad pyramid in youth. As it matures, it becomes rather flat on top, with long outstretched branches covered with old cones and dead branchlets. This tree is a good choice for stabilizing infertile, dry clay soils. In the southern states it has become an important Christmas tree because of its tolerance to hot, dry conditions.

Pinus wallichiana
Himalayan pine

Needles in 5s, 5 to 10 inches long, soft and bending in the middle, bluish green, persisting 3 to 4 years.

Zones 5 to 7 (to 8 on the West Coast).

Slow to moderate growth rate.

50 to 80 feet high, 30 to 50 feet wide.

Himalayan pine is a graceful tree with a broadly pyramidal habit that provides the framework for its slender, arching needles. The long cones are a rich tan color. It should be grown as a specimen, with considerable space allowed for its growth. In cold, blustery winters, needles will brown. A moist, acid, well-drained loam suits it best.

Podocarpus macrophyllus *var.* maki
Shrubby podocarpus

Needles 1 to 2¾ inches long, ¼ to ⅜ inch wide, waxy dark green above, two wide greenish white bands below.

Slow growth rate.

Zones 8 to 10.

20 to 35 feet high, 10 to 15 feet wide.

A beautiful and distinct columnar to oval evergreen that is used for screening, hedging, and espaliers. Often used against walls or fences and pruned to create interesting patterns. On female plants, ½-inch-long, oval, red to reddish purple fruits ripen in August or September. The fruits often have a waxy coat that gives them a bluish color. Shrubby podocarpus tolerates salt spray as well as moderate shade. The beautiful airy foliage is attractive throughout the seasons. Although it grows best in moist, fertile, well-drained soils, it also grows in sand or clay. Temperatures below 0°F result in some foliage damage.

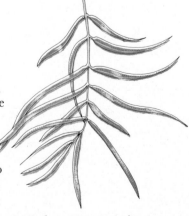

Podocarpus stem tip

Below: *Pseudolarix kaempferi*
Right: *Pseudotsuga menziesii*

Pseudolarix kaempferi
Golden larch

Needles 1½ to 2½ inches long, soft green, turning golden yellow in fall before dropping, needles borne singly on growth of the season, clustered on short side shoots.

Zones 4 to 7 (to 8 on the West Coast).

Slow growth rate.

30 to 50 feet high, 20 to 40 feet wide.

Larch needle attachment

This deciduous conifer has limited zones of adaptability and requires a moist, acid, deep, well-drained soil. Young trees have a broad pyramidal habit. With age, it develops wide-spreading, horizontal branches similar to those of *Cedrus libani*. The cones change from waxy lime green to rich golden brown and shatter after maturity. Golden larch should be used as a specimen or in widely spaced groups.

Pseudotsuga menziesii
Douglas fir

Needles 1 to 1½ inches long, angular in cross section, dark to bluish green, smell of camphor when bruised.

Zones 4 to 6 (to 8 on the West Coast).

Moderate growth rate.

40 to 80 feet high, 12 to 20 feet wide.

When properly grown, not many evergreens can compete effectively for landscape attention with Douglas fir. Gracefully pyramidal in youth, it will maintain this outline for considerable time if soil and atmospheric conditions are favorable. The species is best adapted to the West, but the variety *glauca,* which has bluish green needles, is considered the hardiest and the best adapted to midwestern and eastern conditions. Douglas fir is grown as far south as Atlanta, but it languishes in the heat and seldom makes a respectable specimen. The female cones are interesting; they emerge a rich rose red and later develop hairlike "whiskers." Transplant Douglas fir in spring and provide it with moist, acid, deep, and well-drained soil. It is most effectively used as a specimen, in an informal screen, or as a Christmas tree.

Douglas fir cone

Sciadopitys verticillata
Japanese umbrella-pine

Needles 2 to 5 inches long and ⅛ inch wide, lustrous dark green, borne in a whorl of 20 to 30 at the end of the branch.

Zones 4 to 8.

Slow growth rate.

20 to 30 feet high, 15 to 20 feet wide.

This magnificent evergreen is considered by some experts to be the most handsome and distinctive of all conifers. Despite its name, this is not a true pine. It is, however, an excellent landscape plant. Its dense, broadly pyramidal habit and slow growth

Sciadopitys needle attachment

Sequoia sempervirens

Sequoiadendron giganteum

make it suitable for specimen use. Japanese umbrella-pine has no insect or disease problems. It grows best in soils that are rich, moist, acid, and well drained. In southern areas, locate the plant in light shade.

Redwood stem tip and cone

Sequoia sempervirens
Redwood

Needles ¼ to 1 inch long, dark or bluish green above, two white bands below.
Zones 7 to 9.
Moderate growth rate.
Over 300 feet high in the wild, 60 to 100 feet under cultivation.

The redwood is the tallest tree on earth, occasionally growing to more than 350 feet. Its rich reddish brown bark has deep furrows and high ridges. Although beautiful and imposing in the wild, it is often disappointing in cultivation if planted where it cannot receive abundant, even moisture. With few exceptions, successful culture on the East Coast is almost impossible. In the West, its use should be restricted to areas that most closely resemble the moist, cool growing conditions of its native habitat. When properly grown, however, there is much to recommend it for use in groves or as specimens. Several cultivars have been selected for foliage color and growth habit. 'Soquel', 'Los Altos', and 'Los Gatos' are popular in the West. 'Pendula' and 'Nana Pendula' are grown in the East in rock gardens and rare-conifer gardens with a measure of success.

Sequoiadendron giganteum
Giant sequoia

Needles ½ inch long, sharply pointed, scalelike, two whitish bands above, dark bluish green below.
Zones 6 to 9.
Moderate growth rate.
60 to 90 feet high, 15 to 25 feet wide.

The giant sequoia grows 300 feet tall in the wild but seldom attains more than one-third this size under cultivation. One-hundred-year-old specimens on the East Coast are about 90 feet tall. The habit is pyramidal and the crown full and dense, even in old age. The reddish brown bark is quite attractive. Giant sequoia tolerates dry conditions much better than *Sequoia sempervirens*, but it also prefers moist, acid, deep, and well-drained soils. It does well as a specimen or planted in a grove.

Sequoia stem tip and cone

Taxodium distichum
Bald cypress

Needles ⅓ to ¾ inch long, soft sage green, turn rich brown in fall before they drop.
Zones 5 to 10.
Moderate growth rate.
50 to 70 feet high, 20 to 30 feet wide.

Bald cypress is underrated as a landscape plant. In the wild, this deciduous conifer

Left: *Taxodium distichum*   Below: *Taxus baccata*

Bald cypress cone

grows near slow-moving water or in swamps. It adapts well to drier conditions, however, and can be grown successfully even in the Plains states. As a young tree, it has a columnar growth habit. As it matures, it becomes more wide spreading. The attractive reddish brown bark and uniform branching pattern provide winter interest. New growth appears in late spring, often not until the end of May. The distinctive knees (aboveground roots)

develop on trees planted next to or in water but seldom on trees growing in well-drained soil. Bald cypress looks perfectly at home when planted in low, wet areas or along streams. It also is an excellent grove tree. The wood is particularly rot-resistant; because of its mottled appearance, it is sometimes referred to as pecky cypress. Chlorosis can be a problem for trees grown in alkaline soils.

Taxus
The yews

Yews are long-lived— some specimens have lived more than 1,000 years. They come in all shapes and sizes, from 3-foot ground covers to 60-foot-high trees. The typical foliage color is a lustrous black green, although yellow forms have been selected. Yews do not bear typical cones as other conifers do, but instead produce attractive red berries. The berries, occurring only on female plants, consist of a fleshy

red seed coat, or *aril,* covering a hard seed. The hard seed, the bark, and the leaves contain taxine, a toxic alkaloid, and should not be eaten.

Yews grow in either full sun or shade. They are among the best needle evergreens for shade, superior even to junipers. But they cannot tolerate extremes of temperature and are seldom planted where temperatures drop lower than −20°F or rise above 90°F. Yews prefer moist, acid to neutral, well-drained soil. One of the most significant cultural limitations is excessive moisture. Yews cannot tolerate wet roots, and in fact needle browning may occur after a particularly wet winter or spring. In an area with wet soil, the only way to grow yews is to plant high or use raised beds.
Although yews respond well to pruning, severe uniform pruning leads to a thin shell of foliage on the outside and bare branches inside. When

Yew stem tip and berries

allowed to grow naturally, without pruning, they achieve a beautiful form. Removing half of their new growth with hand pruners each year can also result in a natural, unpruned appearance. Old plants can be cut to within 12 inches of the ground; within 2 or 3 years they will develop into dense, full plants.

Yews have long been used in formal gardens for hedges and topiary. They are also often used as foundation plantings.

Taxus baccata
English yew

Needles ½ to 1½ inch long, somewhat sickle-shaped, lustrous black green.

Taxus × media

Thuja occidentalis

Zones 6 to 7 (to 8 on the West Coast).

Slow growth rate.

35 to 60 feet, 15 to 25 feet wide.

The English yew is a large tree with a broad pyramidal outline. It is the least cold- and heat-tolerant of the yews. 'Fastigiata' (Irish yew) is a cultivar with a distinct rigid, columnar habit. 'Repandens' is a dwarf, wide-spreading form with pendulous branch tips; it grows 2 to 4 feet high and 12 to 15 feet across. This cultivar is probably the hardiest form of English yew and can be grown in zone 5. It is an excellent plant for shade, especially when used on banks or stream edges and allowed to cascade.

Taxus cuspidata
Japanese yew

Needles ½ to 1 inch long, lustrous dark green.

Zones 4 to 7 (to 8 on the West Coast).

Slow growth rate.

Size varies, depending on cultivar.

The Japanese yew is a beautiful, soft-textured, broad, pyramidal tree with rich reddish brown bark. Although the species is not available commercially, cultivars are widely available. 'Capitata', which has extremely dark green needles, is usually trained in a dense pyramidal form. It can be maintained in this fashion with proper pruning. 'Nana' forms a wide-spreading plant about 8 to 10 feet high and 15 to 20 feet wide at maturity. All the cultivars can be maintained at a desired height by proper pruning.

Taxus × media
Anglojap yew

Needles ½ to 1 inch long, lustrous dark green.

Zones 4 to 7 (to 8 on the West Coast).

Slow growth rate.

Size varies, depending on cultivar.

Taxus x media is a hybrid of the English and Japanese yews. It has no typical form, just a variety of cultivars (some indistinguishable from one another) that have been chosen over the years. 'Brownii' is a densely rounded male cultivar that may grow 9 feet high and 12 feet wide in 15 to 20 years if not pruned. 'Densiformis' is a dense shrubby form that grows twice as wide as its height. 'Hatfieldii' is an excellent dense, broad pyramidal male form that may reach 12 feet high and 10 feet wide in 20 years. 'Hicksii' is a popular columnar form that is used for hedges. It may grow 20 feet high after 15 to 20 years. 'Tauntonii', a spreading form about 3 to 4 feet high, is one of the most cold- and heat-tolerant selections. 'Wardii' is an excellent form, with dark green needles and a wide-spreading outline; it may grow 6 feet high and 18 feet wide after 20 years.

Left: *Thuja occidentalis* 'Pendula'
Below: *Thuja orientalis*

Thuja
The arborvitaes

The arborvitaes are not as popular as the junipers and yews, but they are quite valuable in the landscape, providing different colors and textures. They tolerate a wider range of soil conditions than yews, and several species display excellent heat and cold tolerance.

Arborvitaes are a staple in landscapes throughout the country. They are favored for hedge and foundation plantings, although their greatest beauty is shown in groupings or groves.

These plants need full sun; they become open and unkempt in prolonged shade. Arborvitaes are susceptible to few insects and diseases, but they may have problems with mites, bagworms, and several leaf blights.

Thuja occidentalis
American or eastern arborvitae

Needles scalelike and soft to the touch, lustrous medium to dark green, sprays held in a horizontal plane.

Zones 3 to 8.

Slow to moderate growth rate.

40 to 60 feet high, 10 to 15 feet wide.

The American arborvitae may appear as a column or a broad pyramid in the landscape. Because it is usually dense and full to the ground, it is excellent in screens and hedges. The bark is grayish to reddish brown and is most attractive on older specimens that have developed a more open habit. A deep, moist, well-drained soil is ideal, although the plant tolerates most soil conditions—even acid and alkaline soils. In severe cold and strong winds, the needles tend to burn. There are many cultivars. 'Douglasi Aurea' has yellow foliage. 'Hetz Midget' is a dense, globe-shaped form with rich green foliage. 'Nigra' is a dense pyramidal form, to 20 feet in height, that holds its dark green needle color through the winter. 'Pendula' has an attractive, irregular, open pyramidal shape with ascending, arching branches and pendulous branchlets. 'Techny' has dark green needles and a dense, broad pyramidal outline (15 to 20 feet high); it is probably the best selection for northern gardens. 'Woodwardii' is an old variety that grows into a large globe of dark green foliage, which tends to brown in winter.

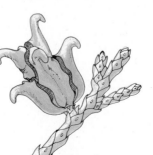

Arborvitae cone

Thuja orientalis (Platycladus orientalis)
Oriental arborvitae

Needles scalelike and soft to the touch, bright grass green, sprays held in a vertical plane, providing a rigid formality.

Zones 5 to 9.

Slow growth rate.

18 to 25 feet high, 10 to 12 feet wide.

In its typical form, *Thuja orientalis* is a large shrub or small tree. When young, it has a stiff, dense, compact, conical or columnar outline. It becomes more loose and open with age. This species is much more tolerant of heat, drought, and alkaline soils than *T. occidentalis*. In northern areas, it should be protected from extreme wind. This species is best adapted to the southern parts of the United States. It is, however, sold in mass-market outlets and is being grown where it has limited chance of

Thuja plicata

Thujopsis dolabrata

ever succeeding. The cultivars are more popular than the species. 'Aurea Nana' ('Berckmans') is a compact, dense, ovoid form with strong vertical sprays and golden yellow foliage. 'Bakeri', which has bright green foliage and a broad conical shape, is well suited to hot, dry climates. 'Westmont' is a compact globe form whose rich dark green foliage is tipped with yellow from spring to fall.

Thuja plicata
Western red cedar

Needles scalelike and soft to the touch, lustrous dark green.
Zones 5 to 7 (to 8 on the West Coast).
Slow to moderate growth rate.
50 to 70 feet high, 15 to 25 feet wide.

Thuja plicata is the most beautiful of all the arborvitaes. In its native Pacific Northwest, it is a massive timber tree, 150 feet and more in height. Its growth habit is distinctly pyramidal in both youth and old age. Trees grow to about 100 feet high under cultivated conditions, retain their lower branches, and appear dense and full throughout the crown. This species appears to be more sensitive to excessive heat and drought than *T. occidentalis* and *T. orientalis*. It is an excellent choice as a specimen or in a screen or grouping.

Thujopsis stem tip

Thujopsis dolabrata
Hiba arborvitae

Needles scalelike and soft to the touch, resembling those of arborvitae, except that underside of sprays is marked with whitish stripes.
Zones 5 to 7 (to 9 on the West Coast).
Slow growth rate.
30 to 50 feet high, 10 to 20 feet wide.

Although *Thujopsis dolabrata* is never really considered for landscape use because of its resemblance to arborvitae and its more stringent cultural requirements, it is nonetheless a beautiful evergreen for specimen use. It prefers a cool, moist climate and moist, rich, acid soil. The dwarf form, 'Nana', is a fine choice for rock gardens and foundation plantings and is more adaptable than the species.

Tsuga
The hemlocks

If only one conifer could be chosen for a garden, the hemlock might be the first choice. There is no finer evergreen for richness of needle color, gracefulness of form, and softness of habit.

Hemlocks are large trees that thrive in cold climates, acid soils, and moderate humidity. They grow well in either sun or shade. Although they present no special transplanting problems, hemlocks should be moved only in spring. With fall transplanting, the plant may not develop enough roots to supply the top with water, and the foliage may burn in a severe winter. In the Midwest, protection from winds is advisable.

Hemlocks are excellent as specimen trees and in groves, and they can be maintained as low hedges indefinitely. They are susceptible to mites, cankers, and other pests, but nothing of an

Tsuga canadensis

Tsuga canadensis 'Sargenti'

epidemic nature. In the Mid-Atlantic states, woolly aphids have proven particularly troublesome in recent years.

Hemlock stem tip and cone

Tsuga canadensis
Canadian hemlock

Needles ¼ to ¾ inch long, lustrous dark green above, two parallel whitish bands below, toothed margins, needles held in relatively flat plane with 180° angle between their surfaces.

Zones 3 to 7 (to 8 on the West Coast).

Moderate growth rate.

40 to 70 feet high, 25 to 35 feet wide.

Canadian hemlock, the aristocrat of conifers, is softly and gracefully pyramidal in youth and becomes pendulously pyramidal with age. The new spring growth is light yellow green before changing to lustrous dark green. A moist, acid, well-drained soil is essential for landscape success. This tree is not tolerant of city conditions or salt pollution. It is excellent as an accent or specimen plant or in a foundation planting, and it has no rivals for screens or hedges. There are a great many cultivars. A commonly available selection is 'Sargenti', which has a magnificent, broadly weeping form.

Tsuga caroliniana
Carolina hemlock

Needles ½ to 1 inch long, glossy dark green above, two distinct whitish bands below, margin smooth, needles radiate around stem, producing a bottlebrush effect.

Zones 4 to 7.

Slow growth rate.

45 to 60 feet high, 20 to 25 feet wide.

The Carolina hemlock is seldom a landscape match for the Canadian hemlock. It is an airy, open, pyramidal tree with short, stout, often semipendulous branches. The soil and climatic requirements are similar to those of *T. canadensis*. Although this tree deserves consideration for specimen use, it is generally difficult to locate commercially.

Tsuga diversifolia
Northern Japanese hemlock

Needles ¼ to ⅝ inch long, lustrous dark green, two narrow white bands below.

Zones 5 and 6.

Slow growth rate.

20 to 30 feet high, 10 to 20 feet wide.

Although it is rare in cultivation, *Tsuga diversifolia* makes a beautiful, graceful broad pyramid. It does not grow as large as the other species, at least in cultivation, but its cultural requirements are similar. It can be effectively used for screening and hedging.

Tsuga heterophylla
Western hemlock

Needles ¼ to 1 inch long, dark green above, two whitish bands below.

Zones 6 to 8.

Fast growth rate.

70 to 100 feet high, 20 to 40 feet wide.

This is the western counterpart of *T. canadensis* and, like that species, requires a cool, moist climate for best growth. Gracefully pyramidal with drooping branchlets, it resembles a well-grown deodar cedar. Although it is not widely used, western hemlock is excellent as a specimen and in screens, hedges, and groupings. Its landscape use should be restricted to the western United States, where it is naturally adapted. Protection from drying winds is also recommended.

Broadleaf evergreens

The broadleaf evergreens encompass a wide variety of plants, all of which produce flowers and fruits and belong to the large group of plants termed angiosperms. Like the needle evergreens, broadleaf evergreens retain all or part of their foliage throughout the year.

Abelia × grandiflora

Abelia × grandiflora
Glossy abelia

Leaves ½ to 1½ inches long, lustrous dark green, becoming purplish bronze in cold weather.

Zones 5 to 9.

Moderate to fast growth rate.

3 to 8 feet high, 3 to 8 feet wide.

The glossy abelia tends to respond like a herbaceous perennial in zones 5 and 6. In cold winters it is often killed back to the snow line but recovers and makes 3 to 4 feet of dense growth in a single season. It blooms on new growth from June or July until frost, producing whitish, pink-tinged, slightly

fragrant, trumpet-shaped flowers. In more southerly areas, glossy abelia grows 6 to 8 feet high and is used for mass plantings and hedges. It displays excellent sun and shade tolerance and will grow in almost any well-drained soil. 'Prostrata' and 'Sherwood' are lower-growing, more compact forms with smaller leaves. 'Francis Mason' is a cultivar with rather sickly yellow foliage.

Abelia 'Edward Goucher' is a hybrid between *A.* x *grandiflora* and *A. schumannii;* its rich purple-pink flowers reflect the influence of the latter parent. 'Edward Goucher' forms an upright arching shrub, 4 to 6 feet high, that can be used for unpruned hedges, bank plantings, or groupings. The foliage is not as lustrous or dark green as that of *A.* x *grandiflora.*

Andromeda polifolia (Kalmia polifolia)
Bog rosemary

Leaves 1 to 1½ inches long, dark green to gray

green, leaf margins roll under.

Zones 2 to 5 (to 7 on the West Coast).

Slow growth rate.

1 to 2 feet high, 2 to 3 feet wide.

This dainty, dapper plant is ideal for a rock garden. The foliage on some forms ('Nana' for one) is a rich, almost bluish green. The urn-shaped, ¼-inch-long, pinkish white flowers appear in small clusters toward the end of May. Soils must be acid, moist, and peaty and temperatures cool. It is worth the effort to provide the proper cultural conditions.

Arctostaphylos uva-ursi
Bearberry, Kinnikinick

Leaves ½ to 1 inch long, lustrous dark green, becoming bronze to reddish in winter.

Zones 2 to 5 (to 9 on the West Coast).

Slow to moderate growth rate.

6 to 12 inches high, 2 to 4 feet wide.

A sandy dune on Cape Cod, a slope along Lake Michigan, a mountainside in the Rocky Mountains, and a Pacific Coast hillside all play host to the bearberry, which grows in cool northern climates throughout the world. Most gardeners consider bearberry strictly an acid-loving species, but it is equally at home on limestone and siliceous rock. It is a low-growing ground cover that eventually forms broad,

Andromeda polifolia

Top left: *Arctostaphylos uva-ursi*
Bottom left: *Aucuba japonica*
Below: *Berberis julianae*

thick mats. The small pinkish white, urn-shaped flowers appear in April or May and are followed by lustrous, bright red fruits, ⅓ inch in diameter, in September or October. It requires good drainage, and grows in full sun or light shade. Once established, it fills in quickly. Several cultivars have been selected and are more common in the West than the Midwest and East.

Aucuba japonica
Japanese aucuba

Leaves 3 to 8 inches long, lustrous dark green, leathery in texture.
Zones 7 to 10.
Slow growth rate.
6 to 10 feet high, usually slightly less in width.

Japanese aucuba is an excellent evergreen for shady, dark corners of the landscape. It is full and dense and should be used in groups or masses for best effect. The small purple flowers appear in March or April. Bright, cherry red, egg-shaped fruits ripen in October and persist through winter. Japanese aucuba grows best in shade, but it tolerates filtered sun, or at most a few hours of morning sun; the leaves of plants in full sun may blacken and die. It thrives in moist, acid, and well-drained soils, but can grow in soils that are less than ideal. 'Nana' is a compact form about half the size of the species. 'Variegata' (gold dust plant) has yellow-flecked leaves and bears abundant red fruits. This selection can be used effectively to brighten dark areas of the landscape.

Berberis julianae
Wintergreen barberry

Leaves 1¼ to 2½ inches long, lustrous dark green, often bronzing or becoming claret in winter, with spiny, toothed edges.
Zones 6 to 8.
Slow to moderate growth rate.
6 to 8 feet high, 6 to 8 feet wide.

When unmarred by pruning shears, the wintergreen barberry makes an excellent dense, rounded evergreen shrub. It fills in nicely without pruning. This thorny species has 3-part spines, which make it suitable for a barrier or loose hedge. The showy, bright yellow flowers appear in April and are followed by grayish blue-black fruits. A well-drained soil is the only requirement for successful culture, but protection from drying winter winds is helpful in northern areas. When temperatures drop below −10° F, the leaves may be killed but the stems usually remain uninjured and put out a new flush of foliage in the spring. 'Nana' is a particularly fine form because of its compact habit, small size (about half the size of the species), and heavy flowering.

Aucuba japonica

Another evergreen barberry that might be grown in areas where *B. julianae* proves successful is *B. candidula*, paleleaf barberry, with a lustrous dark green upper leaf surface and whitish lower surface. It forms a broad mound about 3 feet high.

Arctostaphylos uva-ursi

Berberis julianae

Buxus sempervirens

With winter protection, it is hardy to −5°F. Another species, *B. verruculosa* (warty barberry), is similar to *B. candidula* and is often confused with it. When mature, it ranges from 3 to 6 feet high. It does not appear to be as cold-hardy as *B. candidula*.

Buxus microphylla *var.* koreana
Korean littleleaf boxwood

Leaves ⅓ to 1 inch long, medium green, changing to ugly yellowish brown in winter.
Zones 5 to 9.
Slow growth rate.
3 to 4 feet high, 3 to 4 feet wide.

Korean littleleaf boxwood is the most cold-hardy of all the boxwoods and is grown successfully where temperatures drop to −25°F. The only drawback is its sickly yellowish brown winter color. It has a dense, full growth habit, generally forming broad mounds. Well-drained soil is the only essential cultural requirement. For parterres, hedges, low masses, and groupings, it is a fine choice. The small, cream-colored, fragrant flowers open in March or April and attract bees. 'Tide Hill' and 'Wintergreen' retain their green foliage color in the winter months. 'Wintergreen' is commercially available and should be used in place of the species.

Buxus sempervirens
Common or English boxwood

Leaves ½ to 1¼ inches long, dark green.
Zones 6 to 9.
Slow growth rate.

15 to 20 feet high, 15 to 20 feet wide.
One of the most useful garden plants, the common boxwood has been used for centuries in gardens throughout the world. Left on its own, it becomes dense and full and the branches arch gracefully to form a large mound of dark green foliage. As a hedge plant it has few competitors, since it responds well to pruning. It has no special cultural requirements, but scale, leaf miner, and psyllid may cause problems. It grows somewhat faster than *B. microphylla* var. *koreana* but is not as hardy, although selected cultivars can be grown farther north than the species. Unfortunately, even these will be injured at −15°F and below. Among the best of the hardy clones are 'Inglis', 'Northern Beauty', 'Northern Find', 'Pullman', 'Vardar Valley' (broad, flat-topped form, one of the best but still not perfectly hardy at −15° to −20°F), and 'Welleri'.

Callistemon citrinus

Callistemon citrinus
Lemon bottlebrush

Leaves to 3 inches long, coppery when young, turning to green when mature.
Zones 8 to 10.
Fast growth rate.
15 to 25 feet high, similar or narrower spread.
This tender evergreen is most notable for the showy, bright red, brushlike flowers that it produces periodically throughout the year.

Below: *Camellia japonica*
Top right: *Calluna vulgaris*
Bottom right: *Camellia sasanqua*

Lemon bottlebrush is a vigorous grower that develops into a dense shrub ideal for screens and hedges. Young plants may be trained into espaliers or single- or multiple-trunked accent trees.

Lemon bottlebrush thrives in full sun and moist, well-drained soil. It tolerates drought and heavy soils and is rarely troubled by insects or diseases.

Calluna vulgaris
Scotch heather

Leaves almost needlelike, about ⅛ inch long, rich green.
Zones 4 to 7.
Slow growth rate.

Calluna vulgaris

4 to 24 inches high, makes a broad matlike cover with time.

A field of heather in flower is a most beautiful sight. The rich rosy to purplish pink flowers appear from July to September. Many cultivars have been selected, and flower colors range from white to pink to almost red. The spent flowers should be cut back to encourage shoot growth. Varieties with yellowish or reddish foliage are also available. Heather requires a well-drained, sandy, acid soil and reasonable protection from sweeping winds. Full sun is necessary for maximum flowering.

Camellia japonica
Japanese camellia

Leaves 2 to 4 inches long, lustrous dark green above, lighter beneath, leathery.
Zones 7 to 10.
Slow growth rate.
10 to 15 feet high, 6 to 10 feet wide.

Japanese camellia was once the most popular flowering broadleaf

Camellia japonica

evergreen. The advent of many new broadleaf species and cultivars, as well as the limited cold tolerance of its flower buds, contributed to its decline in popularity. It is rather stiff, rigid, and dense, making it difficult to blend into contemporary landscapes. In addition, the plant requires shade in both summer and winter because the leaves turn yellow in full sun. It grows best in soil that is acid, well-drained, and high in organic matter. Flowers may be single or double and range from white to red, including combinations. They open in November or December and continue blooming into March. Unfortunately, the flowers are easily damaged by cold weather; temperatures near 0° F may kill many of the flower buds. Japanese camellia should be used in the shrub border, in groupings, and perhaps for screening.

Another species, *C. sasanqua,* is more refined in growth habit, foliage, and flower. It will grow 10 to 15 feet high and as wide. The branches are more lax and open than those of *C. japonica.* The small (1½ to 3 inches long), lustrous dark green leaves do not appear as coarse as those of the Japanese species. The 2- to 3-inch-diameter flowers open in September or October and carry into December and beyond. The color range is comparable to that of *C. japonica.* Some cultivars are lightly fragrant. This species is even less cold-hardy than *C. japonica* and is more suitable in zones 8 to 10.

Cotoneaster dammeri

Cleyera japonica

Cleyera japonica

Cleyera japonica
Japanese cleyera

Leaves 2½ to 4 inches long, lustrous dark green in summer, becoming bronzed or wine red in winter, very leathery in texture.

Zones 7 to 9, possibly into 10.

Slow growth rate.

8 to 10 (sometimes 20) feet high, 5 to 6 feet wide.

This handsome and dignified shrub is quite often overpruned. When allowed to fill out naturally, it develops a stratified, layered branching structure. The leaves are clustered at the ends of the branches, creating a Japanese effect. In May or June,

creamy white flowers appear on the previous year's growth. The flowers are subtle but lovely. The red, egg-shaped fruits ripen in September or October and offer excellent color. Japanese cleyera can be used on corners of buildings to soften harsh architectural lines. It makes an excellent screen and can be used as an understory plant in shady locations. It grows best in moist, acid, well-drained soils, but it does tolerate dry soils. 'Variegata' has marbeled gray leaves with a creamy white to yellowish margin that turns rose pink with the advent of cold weather.

Cotoneaster dammeri
Bearberry cotoneaster

Leaves ¾ to 1½ inches long, lustrous dark green, often developing a reddish purple tinge in cold weather.

Zones 5 to 9.

Fast growth rate.

1 to 3 feet high, 6 feet wide.

The evergreen cotoneasters are choice landscape plants, but most have proven to be minimally cold-hardy. The bearberry cotoneaster is one of the most cold- and heat-tolerant species. The white flowers that appear in May or June are attractive and are followed by rich red fruits. The species is adaptable to acid and alkaline soils, but it must have good drainage. For ground-cover use in full sun or partial shade, the bearberry cotoneaster has much to offer. It grows extremely fast and will provide complete cover in a single growing season when spaced 2½ to 3 feet apart. Several good selections are available. 'Coral Beauty' ('Royal Beauty') has lustrous

Cotoneaster dammeri

dark green foliage and abundant red fruits. 'Skogholm', the most popular form, grows extremely fast but does not fruit to the degree of 'Coral Beauty'. These cotoneasters are relatively free of fire blight, mites, and leaf tier, which are troublesome on other species.

Another small-leaved evergreen species is *C. congestus* (Pyrenees cotoneaster), which grows 1½ to 2½ feet high and forms a spreading, rounded, compact mass resembling a small haystack. The small, dull bluish green leaves, pinkish white flowers, and ¼-inch-diameter fruits are attractive. It is an excellent rock garden plant that is best grown in zones 6 to 8. Fire blight can be a problem on this species.

Cotoneaster conspicuus (wintergreen cotoneaster) is a small-leaved (¼ inch long), prostrate or spreading evergreen shrub of variable size. In some forms it seldom grows over 4 feet high,

Below: *Cotoneaster microphyllus* 'Cochleatus'
Right: *Daphne cneorum* 'Variegata'

and in others it reaches 8 to 10 feet. The ⅜-inch-diameter white flowers are followed by abundant bright scarlet round fruits of the same diameter. Birds do not seem to be attracted to the fruit, and it often persists through the winter. *Cotoneaster microphyllus* (littleleaf cotoneaster) is a low, spreading or even prostrate evergreen shrub, rarely more than 2 or 3 feet high. The ½-inch-long leaves are lustrous dark green above and coated with woolly hairs below. The white flowers and red fruits are similar to those of *C. conspicuus*.

Cotoneaster salicifolius
Willowleaf cotoneaster

Leaves 1½ to 3½ inches long, lustrous dark green above, often with white woolly hairs below.

Zones 6 to 9.

Fast growth rate.

10 to 15 feet high, usually wider than high.

Willowleaf cotoneaster is a handsome shrub, especially when adorned with masses of red fruits. The white flowers have a curious and rather objectionable odor similar to that of the hawthorns. It makes a valuable contribution in groupings or in the shrub border. The species is not widely used because of problems with fire blight and mites. The variety *C. s.* var. *floccosus* is more common in cultivation; it tends to be semievergreen farther north. Excellent low-growing evergreen cultivars that are useful as ground covers include 'Autumn Fire', 'Gnom', 'Parkteppich', 'Repens', 'Saldam', and 'Scarlet Leader'. All have lustrous dark green leaves that are considerably smaller than those of the species. They grow no more than 1½ feet high and show increased resistance to fire blight. 'Scarlet Leader' has proven outstanding in the heat of the South, and

'Repens' is widely used in the North.

None of the other evergreen cotoneaster species—such as *C. frigidus* (Himalayan cotoneaster), *C. lacteus* (milky cotoneaster), and *C.* x *watereri* (waterer cotoneaster)—are hardy enough to warrant consideration above zone 7. Even then, they are poorly adapted to the heat and humidity of the South.

Daphne cneorum
Garland or rose daphne

Leaves ¾ to 1 inch long, very narrow, lustrous dark green, attractive throughout the year.

Zones 4 to 7 (to 8 on the West Coast).

Slow growth rate.

6 to 12 inches high, 2 feet wide or more.

This wonderful garden gem is one of the finest of all plants for rock gardens. It makes an excellent ground cover in full sun or light shade but should not be expected to

Daphne odora 'Aureomarginata'

cover large areas. Delightfully fragrant rose pink flowers cover the plant during May. Very few ground-cover species can equal the floral display of this wonderful plant. Rose daphne should be transplanted in the spring into well-drained, moist, near neutral (pH 6 to 7) soil. The plants don't tolerate disturbance and should be left in place once established. 'Alba' is a white-flowered form. 'Variegata' has beautiful, dainty, cream-edged leaves and rose pink flowers.

Daphne odora
Winter daphne

Leaves 1½ to 3½ inches long, ½ to 1 inch wide, lustrous dark green.
Zones 7 to 9.
Slow growth rate.
3 to 4 feet high, 3 to 4 feet wide.

Winter daphne is appropriately named for the rosy purple flowers that appear from late January to March. The flowers are borne on the ends of the branches on this robust, broad, rounded shrub. Their fragrance is so strong that several plants will scent a small garden. This species prefers partial shade. It is not very cold-hardy, and flower buds may be killed at 0° F. 'Alba' has white flowers, and 'Aureomarginata' has faintly yellow-margined leaves.

Elaeagnus pungens

Elaeagnus pungens
Thorny elaeagnus, silverberry

Leaves 2 to 4 inches long, gray green above, covered with silvery brown scales below.

Zones 7 to 10.
Fast growth rate.
10 to 15 feet high, 10 to 15 feet wide.

Thorny elaeagnus is a fast-growing and aggressive broadleaf evergreen. Once it it is established in a new area, it soon becomes the dominant shrub. Its growth habit is spreading, but long shoots wander in disarray from all parts of the plant. It is often used for screening along highways and for hiding undesirable buildings and structures. When pruned and kept in check, it makes an effective hedge. This shrub will grow in virtually any soil that is not permanently wet.

Because the species is able to convert atmospheric nitrogen into a form suitable for its own use, it can thrive in infertile, inhospitable soils. The silvery white, trumpet-shaped, fragrant flowers appear in October or November. The scaly red fruit ripens in April or May and serves as food for birds. Many cultivars have been named. The most common are 'Maculata', whose leaves have a variable deep yellow blotch in the center, and 'Simonii', which has larger, more silvery leaves and a more subdued growth habit.

Erica herbacea
(Erica carnea)
Spring heath

Leaves needlelike, small, and in clusters around the stem.
Zones 4 to 7 (to 8 on the West Coast).
Slow growth rate.
8 to 12 inches high, 18 inches wide.

Spring heath is one of the most popular heaths in American gardens. It forms a compact mound or cushion that is densely covered with rich green leaves. From January through March the plant comes alive with rose red, urn-shaped flowers. The flowers are present for a month or more and can be spectacular. Spring heath looks good when massed together or when planted in the rock garden. Heaths require an acid, moist, well-drained soil with lots of organic matter. Spent flowers should be removed to prolong blooming. 'Springwood White' and 'Springwood Pink' are commonly available cultivars of considerable merit.

Erica herbacea

Below: *Escallonia rubra*
Right: *Eriobotrya japonica*
Far right: *Eucalyptus globulus*

Eriobotrya japonica

Erica cinerea (bell heath), *E. tetralix* (crossleaf heath), and *E. vagans* (Cornish heath) flower in summer or fall and offer shades of pink and purple.

Eriobotrya japonica
Loquat

Leaves 6 to 9 inches long, 3 to 4 inches wide, lustrous dark green above, covered with brown hairs below, new leaves bronze to red.
Zones 8 to 10.
Moderate growth rate.
15 to 25 feet high, 15 to 25 feet wide.

Loquat is quite effective when grown as a small evergreen tree and used as an accent or focal point. The large leaves attract immediate visual attention, so proper siting is critical. Loquat makes an effective espalier on large expanses of brick. The off-white, fragrant flowers open anytime from November to January, and the edible yellow fruits ripen in April and later. Loquat prefers a moist, well-drained soil, but it will grow in sand or clay. To prevent winter injury in areas where temperatures drop to 0° F, plant loquat in courtyards, coves, or other protected locations. Fire blight can be a problem.

Escallonia rubra
Red escallonia

Leaves 2 to 3 inches long, deep glossy green, fine-toothed edges.
Zones 8 to 10.
Fast growth rate.
6 to 15 feet high, similar or slightly narrower spread.

Escallonia rubra

Red escallonia is a tender shrub or small tree with a dense, rounded, upright growth habit. It does well in mild coastal areas. It bears red or rose red flowers in the early summer to early fall. Escallonia makes a good hedge, screen, or shrub border. It is extremely vigorous and requires a firm hand with the pruners to keep it in bounds.

Red escallonia needs light shade or filtered sun, or full sun in coastal areas. It tolerates most soils as long as drainage is adequate, and it is not particularly susceptible to pests or diseases. Several cultivars are available.

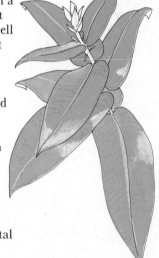

Eucalyptus globulus

Eucalyptus globulus
Blue gum

Leaves 6 to 12 inches long, 1½ inches wide, waxy, blue gray, aromatic.
Zones 9 to 10.
Fast growth rate.
75 to 100 feet high, narrower spread.

Blue gum is one of the most widely cultivated members of the *Eucalyptus* genus. Like almost all eucalypts, blue gum is native to

Below: *Eucalyptus ficifolia*
Right: *Euonymus fortunei*

Australia. This fast-growing, shallow-rooted plant develops into a straight-trunked, tall, columnar, graceful tree with a striking silhouette. It bears creamy white to yellow flowers that develop into hard, blue gray seed capsules. Blue gum is often used as a screen or windbreak. It thrives in a mild, warm climate and does best in a deep, well-drained soil.

Although it is one of the most commonly planted eucalypts, blue gum has several disadvantages. It grows very rapidly and needs a large landscape to accommodate its eventual size, and it is a messy plant, littering the ground around it with seed capsules, bark, leaves, and dangerously large branches. Several other species are better suited to most landscapes. *E. citriodora* (lemon-scented gum) is a tall, slender, graceful tree that tolerates a variety of soil types. *E. ficifolia* (red-flowering gum) is a small, bushy tree that grows to 25 feet and bears striking, deep red flowers. *E. gunnii* (cider gum) is one of the hardiest of the eucalypts, tolerating temperatures as low as 5° F. *E. polyanthemos* (the silver dollar gum), an attractive single- or multistemmed tree, bears striking round, silvery foliage as a young tree. *E. sideroxylon* (red ironbark) is a fast-growing tree with deeply furrowed, nonshedding, nearly black bark.

Euonymus fortunei
Wintercreeper euonymus

Leaf size varies, depending on cultivar, from ¼ inch to more than 2 inches long.
Zones 4 to 9, needs snow cover or protection in zone 4.

Fast growth rate, depending somewhat on cultivar.
Size varies, depending on culture.

The wintercreeper euonymus is a variable species that has given rise to numerous cultivars. The inconspicuous greenish white flowers develop into orange red seeds that are attractive but are produced in abundance on just a few of the cultivars (var. *radicans*, 'Carrierei', 'Sarcoxie', var. *vegeta*, and 'Woodland'). There are no special soil considerations other than good drainage. They tolerate full sun or heavy shade. Cultivars of wintercreeper euonymus can be used for ground covers, groupings, low hedges, and wall coverings. The variegated types are effective in dark corners and heavily shaded areas. The vining types produce rootlike holdfasts with which they attach themselves to brick, stone, and other suitable materials; they are excellent wall covers.

All are easily rooted from cuttings.

Here are a few of the more common and better cultivars.

■ 'Colorata': Vigorous ground-cover form with glossy deep green leaves that turn plum purple in winter. Grows 12 inches high.

■ 'Dart's Blanket': An improvement on 'Colorata', with 1- to 2-inch-long, waxy, dark green leaves and a bronzed to reddish purple tint in autumn and winter. Grows 16 inches high.

■ 'Emerald Gaiety': Rounded leaves, ¾ to 1¾ inches in diameter, with pronounced irregular whitish margins that become pinkish in winter. Grows 4 to 5 feet high.

■ 'Golden Prince': A vigorous, mounded form with new foliage tipped bright gold. The older leaves turn solid green. It is considered the hardiest of all variegated *E. fortunei* types. Grows 1 to 2 feet high.

Euonymus fortunei

Left: *Euonymus kiautschovica* 'Manhattan'
Below: *Fatsia japonica*

■ 'Kewensis', 'Longwood', 'Minimus': All are low-growing forms with leaves in the range of ¼ to ½ inch long. 'Kewensis' has the smallest leaves.

■ 'Sarcoxie': An old upright form, 4 feet high, with glossy 1-inch-long leaves. It may set abundant fruits.

■ 'Sun Spot': This rounded, compact form displays good winter hardiness and thick green leaves with blotched yellow centers.

■ Var. *vegeta:* One of the most common forms in cultivation. The shrubby habit (4 to 5 feet high) and rounded, thickish, medium green leaves are unique to this cultivar. It is a heavy fruiter.

All the *E. fortunei* cultivars are susceptible to the damaging euonymus scale, which may be an important consideration when choosing plants for the landscape. Var. *vegeta,* 'Sarcoxie', and 'Colorata' appear to be especially susceptible. If they are not protected from snow in cold winters, the leaves may turn brown. Usually the stems and buds are not injured and the plant comes back.

Euonymus kiautschovicas
Spreading euonymus

Leaves 2 to 3 inches long, up to 1¾ inches wide, lustrous dark green.

Zones 5 to 8.

Moderate to fast growth rate.

8 to 10 feet high, 8 to 10 feet wide.

This species is often chosen when a tough, durable, serviceable shrub is needed for the landscape. It makes an excellent background plant, screen, or hedge. Spreading euonymus may remain evergreen in northern gardens, but when temperatures drop below −10° F the leaves usually turn light brown. It is an extremely adaptable species and will grow in any well-drained soil. The greenish white flowers appear in July and August and have a curious vinegary odor that attracts hordes of flies. It should never be used near patios or in high-traffic areas. The pinkish fruit capsule opens to expose orange-red seeds in October or November. 'Manhattan' is an excellent fast-growing cultivar with glossy dark green leaves; it reaches a height of 4 to 6 feet. It is less cold-hardy than the species.

Fatsia japonica
Japanese fatsia

Leaves 6 to 14 inches across, 7 to 9 lobes, lustrous dark green.

Zones 8 to 10.

Moderate growth rate.

6 to 10 feet high, 6 to 10 feet wide.

If one plant could be chosen for a bold, brash textural effect, Japanese fatsia would be high on the list. The large, rich green leaves are distinctly tropical in effect. For breaking up monotonous areas of the garden, for container or tub planting, or for grouping, this is an excellent choice. The creamy white flowers appear in 18-inch-diameter clusters during October or November and are followed by fleshy black fruits. The species only flowers and fruits in zones 9 and 10. In zone 8, the leaves and stems may be injured unless protected. Japanese fatsia requires filtered sun or full shade, protection from excessive wind, and moist, acid, rich, well-drained soil.

A related species, x *Fatshedera lizei*, is

Fatsia japonica

an intergeneric hybrid between *Fatsia japonica* 'Moseri' and *Hedera helix* 'Hibernica'. It forms a semiclimbing evergreen shrub or vine and is useful for shady locations. Its leathery, lustrous dark green leaves are 4 to 10 inches across and divided into five lobes. It provides excellent textural effects

Below: *Feijoa sellowiana*
Right: *Gardenia jasminoides*

when espaliered or trained on a wall or trellis. Cultural requirements are similar to those of *F. japonica,* but it does offer greater cold-hardiness.

Feijoa sellowiana
Pineapple guava

Leaves 1 to 3 inches long, dark almost bluish green above, covered with dense white hairs below, extremely handsome leaf color.

Zones 8 to 10.

Moderate growth rate.

Feijoa sellowiana

10 to 15 feet high, 10 to 15 feet wide.

This is a marvelous shrub for foliage effect. Even if it had nothing else to offer, it would still rank as a choice ornamental. For massing, hedging, screening, or simply providing a different foliage effect in a shrub border, it is excellent. The flowers are composed of fleshy petals that are red in the center and white around the margins; the petals surround a tuft of bright red filaments (stamens). The flowers appear in June on the current year's shoots. A yellow, egg-shaped, tasty fruit ripens in late summer and early fall. Pineapple guava prefers well-drained, light, loamy soil and full sun. It is quite tolerant of salt spray. Cold is its biggest enemy, and temperatures below 10°F will cause some leaf and stem injury.

Gardenia jasminoides

Gardenia jasminoides
Gardenia

Leaves 2 to 4 inches long, bright, shiny green.

Zones 8 to 10.

Medium growth rate.

2 to 6 feet high, 2 to 6 feet wide.

Gardenias are well known for their heavily fragrant flowers. Depending on the variety, the plants bear their creamy white flowers in late spring through summer. A number of cultivars have been developed, providing variety in plant height and flower size.

Gardenias are versatile shrubs; their attractive foliage and pleasing habit make them useful as

container plants, specimen shrubs, low screens, and espaliers.

Gardenias thrive in hot climates. They need slightly acid, moist soil with good drainage. In coastal areas, give them full sun; inland, provide partial shade. They develop iron chlorosis readily if grown in alkaline soil and require sprays of iron chelate. They are plagued by thrips and whiteflies.

Gaylussacia brachycera
Box huckleberry

Leaves ¾ to 1 inch long, lustrous dark green, turning bronze to reddish purple in winter.

Zones 5 to 7.

Slow growth rate.

12 to 18 inches high, spreading indefinitely.

For some unknown reason this pretty evergreen ground-cover species has never become popular. The white to pinkish flowers appear in May through June and may be followed by bluish fruits in August. It makes an excellent

Left: *Gelsemium sempervirens*   Below: *Hedera helix*

Gaylussacia brachycera

companion plant with other species in the heather family because it demands an acid, well-drained soil high in organic matter. For ground-cover use under pine trees or in other partially shaded situations, it is a good choice. In full sun, the tips of the branches and leaves become reddish.

Gelsemium sempervirens
Carolina jessamine

Leaves 1 to 3¾ inches long, lustrous dark green in summer, often assuming a yellow green cast in winter.

Zones 6 to 9.

Fast growth rate.

10 to 20 feet high.

Carolina jessamine brightens up the spring landscape with its fragrant, vibrant yellow, trumpet-shaped flowers, which appear in great profusion from March through April. It is a twining evergreen vine that will climb up trees and over fences and rock piles, or simply serve as an irregular ground cover. It grows best in full sun, but it will tolerate moderate shade. It will grow in virtually any soil. 'Pride of Augusta' is a double-flowered form.

Gelsemium sempervirens

All parts of the plant are poisonous.

Hedera helix
English ivy

Leaves have 3 to 5 lobes (similar to maple), 2 to 4 inches long and wide, dark green and lustrous above, often with whitish veins creating a mosaic pattern.

Zones 5 to 9.

Fast growth rate.

6 to 8 inches high when used as a ground cover, spreading indefinitely. (Can climb to 90 feet as a vine.)

English ivy has proven to be one of the most functional of all ground-cover and vining plants. No plant is better adapted to shade; it is an excellent choice for those dark, shadowy corners of the landscape. In addition, it will climb almost any surface without support. The stems develop rootlike holdfasts that grow into crevices and pores, "cementing" the plant to the structure. As the plant climbs, the leaves change shape and lose the

Hedera helix

3- to 5-lobed shape. This phase is referred to as the adult form. This form also flowers in the fall and produces round, blackish, poisonous fruits. When propagated by cuttings, this form makes a 4- to 5-foot-high broadleaf evergreen shrub. Several cold-hardy cultivars are 'Baltica', 'Thorndale', and 'Wilson'.

There are hundreds of English ivy cultivars. Ivy is not susceptible to any serious insect or disease problems, and it tolerates extremes of soil.

Iberis sempervirens

Iberis sempervirens
Candytuft

Leaves ½ to 1 inch long, dark green.

Zones 4 to 9.

Slow growth rate.

6 to 12 inches high, 2 to 3 feet wide.

Candytuft, although seldom considered a true broadleaf evergreen, is one of the most functional and beautiful ground-cover evergreens available. As a foreground plant in the shrub border or in a foundation planting, it offers excellent dark green, matlike foliage. For 4 to 6 weeks, in April and May, it is covered with tiny white flowers. The flowers should be removed once they have declined so the new foliage can develop. Pruning shears can make quick work of spent flower heads. Candytuft prefers acid, moist, loamy soil and full sun, but it will grow almost anywhere as long as adequate moisture and fertility are present. It is a great plant to use for softening the vibrant and often contrasting colors of spring bulbs and wild flowers.

Ilex
The hollies

The hollies include several hundred species of deciduous and evergreen trees and shrubs. Most of the evergreen hollies are classic, dependable landscape plants that provide shiny green foliage and brightly colored berries. Hundreds of varieties have been developed, expanding even more the landscape versatility of this plant group. Only the female plants produce berries, but most species require a nearby male holly plant as a pollinator.

Hollies fit nicely into almost any landscape setting. Many are good foundation plants, groupings, or shrub border plants. Some are ideal for barriers, hedges, or informal screens, and a number of them can be effectively used as accent or patio trees.

Most of the evergreen hollies are hardy to zone 7, and many tolerate colder climates. Hollies prefer a cool, moist climate and rich, acid, moist but well-drained soil. A few hollies tolerate drier, warmer conditions. They grow in either sun or shade but are more fruitful and compact in full sun. Hollies are host to several serious pests and diseases, including holly leaf miners, scales, and leaf spots.

Ilex aquifolium
English holly

Leaves 1 to 3 inches long, lustrous dark green,

Ilex aquifolium

margins usually spiny.

Zones 7 to 9.

Slow growth rate.

20 to 30 feet high, 10 to 15 feet wide.

The English holly is a magnificent landscape plant. It forms a dense, broad pyramidal outline at maturity. The dull, creamy flowers are followed by glistening red fruits on the female plants that persist through the winter months. It is quite useful in groupings or as a background for a shrub or perennial border. This species is more sensitive to extreme heat and cold and grows best in a more even climate than that of the East Coast. It succeeds admirably on the Pacific Coast. Numerous cultivars have variegated foliage,

Ilex cornuta 'rotunda'

Ilex cornuta 'rotunda'

large fruits, unusual habit, and increased cold-hardiness. 'Balkans', 'Boulder Creek', and 'Zero' ('Teufel's Weeping') are at least a zone hardier than the species.

Ilex × attenuata 'Foster's No. 2'
Foster's holly

Leaves 1½ to 3 inches long, smooth leaf margins or toothed toward end of leaf, lustrous dark green.

Zones 6 to 9.

Moderate growth rate.

20 to 30 feet high, 8 to 12 feet wide.

E. E. Foster of Bessemer, Alabama, originally developed 5 selections. The only survivor is No. 2, a narrowly conical tree that bears abundant quantities of ¼-inch-diameter bright red fruits. Its texture is finer than that of the Chinese and American hollies. It is particularly effective in groupings but can also be used as an accent plant. The fruits remain on the plant into winter, depending on weather conditions and bird populations. Foster's holly sets fruit without a male pollinator, which means that a single plant can produce a quantity of bright red fruits. Well-drained, moist, acid soil is sufficient.

Ilex cornuta
Chinese holly

Leaves 1½ to 4 inches long, lustrous dark green above, yellow green below, with 5 prominent spines.

Zones 7 to 9 (6 if protected).

Slow growth rate.

10 to 15 feet high, 10 to 15 feet wide.

For all practical purposes, the species is not found commercially; it is represented only by the cultivars. Chinese holly is amazingly tolerant of different soils and climates. It is probably the best holly species for heat and drought tolerance. Low temperatures, near −10° F, cause the plant to lose its leaves. All cultivars can be used for massing, foundation planting, grouping, and hedges, but pruning removes many potential berries. The bright red fruits that occur on female plants average ¼ inch in diameter, but the berries often don't ripen in the cool summers of the Pacific Northwest. 'Burfordii' grows 10 to 20 feet high and to a similar width. The leaves have a single spine at their tip. This is a female plant that produces abundant bright red fruits without the aid of a male for pollination. 'Dwarf Burford' is a smaller version that is better suited to contemporary landscapes. 'Carissa' has a single terminal spine and grows only 3 to 4 feet high and 4 to 6 feet wide. It is an extremely dense form, excellent for massing. 'Dazzler', which has 5-spined leaves, grows about 10 feet high and produces abundant crops of large bright red berries. 'Rotunda' has 5- to 7-spined leaves and forms an impenetrable thicket about 3 to 4 feet high and 6 to 8 feet wide. It is excellent for low hedges and barriers.

Ilex crenata
Japanese holly

Leaves ½ to 1¼ inch long, often lustrous dark green above, yellowish green below, and covered with black dots (glands).

Zones 5 to 9.

Slow growth rate.

Size varies, depending on the cultivar; average is 5 to 10 feet high and wide.

The Japanese holly is one of the most widely used broadleaf evergreens for foundation planting, massing, and hedging. In Japan, hedges have been maintained for so long that they can actually be walked on. The whitish flowers appear in May or June and may be followed by blackish fruits. The fruits tend to be hidden by the foliage and do not make much of a show. Japanese hollies transplant readily; they grow best in a moist, acid, well-drained soil. Waterlogged, heavy soils and alkaline soils result in plant decline. Nematodes may be a problem in the southern states.

Left: *Ilex glabra* 'Compacta'   Below: *Ilex latifolia*

At least 380 cultivars are described in the literature; 60 are available commercially. Here are a few of the best and most cold-hardy. 'Border Gem' has a dense, compact habit and lustrous dark green foliage; it has survived to −8°F. 'Convexa' is considered one of the hardiest forms. It may grow 8 to 10 feet high and twice as wide. The ½-inch-long, lustrous dark green leaves are cupped rather than flat. This is a female clone that is often heavily laden with black fruits. 'Helleri' is a very common form with small leaves that lack the luster of 'Convexa' and others. It is dense, mounded, and spreading, and may ultimately reach a height of about 3 to 4 feet after many years. 'Highlander' is a 6-foot-high, loose, pyramidal form that displays excellent cold tolerance. 'Microphylla' is an upright shrub (10 feet high) that is hardy to zone 5.

Ilex glabra
Inkberry

Leaves 1 to 2 inches long, lustrous dark green, with a few serrations at the end of the leaf.

Zones 4 to 9.

Slow growth rate.

6 to 8 feet high, 8 to 10 feet wide.

This species is one of the few hollies that suckers and forms rather large, billowy plant clumps. Its principal use is as a foliage mass. Although its black fruits are hidden by the leaves, they are more showy than those of *I. crenata*. In general, the plant has a more lax, open habit than *I. crenata*, yet it can be used for an effective screen. It should never be pruned into a hedge. This is the most cold-hardy of the shrubby evergreen hollies, but leaves will burn and drop in severe winters (−20°F and below). 'Compacta' is a dwarf (4 to 5 feet high) female form with denser branches than the species.

A new selection, 'Nordic', is even more compact and does not become leggy and open at the base. The species and cultivars are excellent choices for moist—even wet—soils and should be used in preference to other evergreen hollies for those conditions.

Ilex latifolia
Lusterleaf holly

Leaves 4 to 8 inches long, 1½ to 3 inches wide, lustrous dark green above, yellowish green below.

Zones 7 to 9.

Medium growth rate.

20 to 25 feet high, 10 to 15 feet wide.

Even if this holly never fruited, it would still warrant use in contemporary landscapes because of its beautiful foliage and striking, bold texture. It is broadly pyramidal, but not as full and dense and therefore not as formal as 'Nellie R. Stevens'. The deep red, ⅓-inch-diameter fruits are borne in dense

clusters at the bases of the leaves and almost completely encircle the stem. It has much to offer for formal use, in groupings, or as a background plant. It is very tolerant of heat and drought but will suffer some injury when temperatures drop below 0°F. 'Wirt L. Winn' is a female form resulting from a cross between *I. aquifolium* and *I. latifolia*. The leaves are more lustrous than those of *I. latifolia,* and it produces red fruits in abundance.

Ilex 'Nellie R. Stevens'
Nellie R. Stevens holly

Leaves 1½ to 3½ inches long, leathery, lustrous dark green with 2 to 3 teeth on each side of the leaf margin.

Zones 6 to 9.

Moderate growth rate.

15 to 25 feet high, 10 to 15 feet wide.

'Nellie R. Stevens' is a hybrid resulting from a cross between *I. aquifolium* and *I. cornuta*. It embodies

Below: *Ilex* 'Nellie R. Stevens'   Right: *Ilex opaca*

the excellent foliage and fruit characteristics of the first parent and the tolerance to drought and heat of the latter. Since *I. aquifolium* cannot be grown with any measure of success in most parts of the United States, 'Nellie R. Stevens' serves as a suitable substitute. Its growth habit is broadly pyramidal and rather formal; it can be effectively used in groupings or as a background for shrubs or herbaceous borders. With its rich foliage, it is a match for any other evergreen. The bright red fruits ripen in fall and often persist into winter. A male plant is not required for fruit set. 'Nellie R. Stevens' has excellent heat and drought tolerance but has been killed to the ground at −15° to −18°F.

Ilex × meserveae
Meserve hollies

Leaves 1 to 2½ inches long, lustrous dark green, almost blue green, with spiny margins.

Zones 4 to 8.
Slow growth rate.
Size varies, averages 10 to 15 feet high.
Mrs. Kathleen Meserve received the American Horticultural Society's citation for outstanding contributions to amateur horticulture for breeding and introducing this most important group of cold-hardy shrubby hollies. All were chosen because of good foliage, fruit, and hardiness. A few of the early introductions ('Blue Girl', 'Blue Boy', and 'Blue Angel') are no longer cultivated, but 'Blue Prince' (an excellent male form) and 'Blue Princess' (female) have proven outstanding. 'Blue Maid' forms a broad pyramid, carries a good crop of red fruits, and is considered the hardiest of the lot. 'Blue Stallion', 'China Boy', and 'China Girl' are newer selections that have not had time to prove themselves. The new cultivars should be tested in a given geographic area before large plantings are made.

All the Meserve hollies are good as foundation plants, in groupings, or as shrub border plants. They do not have the formality of the large types and should be looked upon as shrubs instead of trees. Any well-drained acid soil is suitable. Interestingly, these selections appear more drought-tolerant than the average holly.

Ilex opaca
American holly

Leaves 2 to 4 inches long, dull dark green in most forms, often with large spiny teeth around the margin.
Zones 5 to 9.
Slow growth rate.
15 to 30 feet high, 8 to 15 feet wide.
The American holly receives possibly more attention than any other species, but it is certainly not the most impressive of the large-growing, red-berried species. In its finest form, it is densely pyramidal, with branches to the ground. Many

cultivars (at least 1,000 named) have been described; the best selections are those that fruit abundantly and have lustrous dark green foliage. Many cultivars have been selected on a regional basis, and it is wise to check with a local nursery for the best cultivars in a given area. American holly requires a moist, well-drained, acid soil with above-average fertility. Excess wind exposure, inadequate drainage, and alkaline soils must be avoided. Leaf miner and scale are two serious pests.

American holly is best suited as a background plant or in groupings. One male plant to every three females is necessary for pollination and good fruit set.

Ilex pedunculosa
Longstalk holly

Leaves 1 to 3 inches long, lustrous dark green, wavy leaf surface, no spines or serrations on the leaf edges.

Below: *Ilex pedunculosa*   **Right:** *Kalmia latifolia*

Zones 5 to 8.

Slow growth rate.

20 to 30 feet high, 10 to 15 feet wide.

Because cold-hardy, red-fruited hollies with lustrous leaves are rare, *I. pedunculosa* deserves greater landscape consideration. It is dense but still sufficiently loose to show some grace. The brilliant red fruits occur singly on 1- to 2-inch gracefully arching stalks. The fruits, like those of most hollies, ripen in October and are a favorite food for many birds. The species can be used as an informal screen, in groupings, or as an accent plant. It is a good choice for inclusion in the shrub border or the back of the perennial border. Soils should be moist, acid, and well drained. In terms of cold-hardiness, it is probably second only to *I. glabra* and can withstand −15° to −20° F without injury. It also has good wind tolerance.

Ilex vomitoria
Yaupon holly

Leaves ½ to 1½ inches long, lustrous dark green.

Zones 7 to 10.

Slow to moderate growth rate.

15 to 20 feet high, 15 to 20 feet wide.

Yaupon holly is found in most of the coastal area in the United States. It is a large multistemmed shrub or small tree with a very irregular branching pattern. The translucent red fruits occur in great quantities on female plants and remain attractive throughout winter. This species grows in wet or dry soils and is completely tolerant of salt spray. It makes an excellent informal screen or grouping and can be used as an accent plant or patio tree. It can also be fashioned into hedges and unusual topiary. Often the lower branches are removed and the upper branches pruned into an umbrella shape or geometric outline. Male and female weeping forms can be used as accents. The cultivars 'Nana' and 'Schelling's Dwarf' are compact, rounded forms, 3 to 5 feet high, that are used for massing, hedging, and foundation planting.

Kalmia latifolia
Mountain laurel

Leaves 5 inches long, usually lustrous dark green.

Zones 4 to 9.

Slow growth rate.

8 to 15 feet high, similar spread.

Mountain laurel is a large, robust shrub that is symmetrical and dense if not crowded. The new foliage is a bright yellow green that matures to dark green. The flowers are among the most beautiful of all flowering plants, with rich pink buds that open to whitish pink. The flowers occur in large clusters, 4 to 6 inches in diameter, in late May and June. Many selections are available, with flower color ranging from white to almost red.

Mountain laurel requires an acid, cool, moist, well-drained soil and partial shade for best growth. It is almost impossible to grow this plant in heavy clay and alkaline soils. This is an excellent evergreen for shady borders and masses and for naturalizing, but it requires careful attention for best growth. The species is native from Maine to Florida. In the southern part of its range it is found only along watercourses, and it is not likely to survive if moved to a typical southern landscape situation.

Kalmia latifolia

Leucothoe fontanesiana

Leucothoe populifolia

Laurus nobilis

Although mountain laurel has no serious problems, leaf spot may necessitate a spraying program.

Laurus nobilis
Sweet bay

Leaves 3 to 4 inches long, dark glossy green, aromatic.

Zones 8 to 10.

Slow growth rate.

12 to 40 feet high, narrower in spread.

Sweet bay is the ancient laurel of the Greeks and Romans. It is a well-behaved tree or shrub with a naturally dense, compact, columnar growth habit that lends itself to formal garden designs. It produces tiny, inconspicuous yellow flowers that are followed by small, dark fruits. Sweet bay can be grown as a shrub or trained into a single- or multiple-trunked accent or specimen tree. It responds well to shearing, and when clipped it makes a handsome, neat hedge, screen, accent shrub, or topiary. The aromatic leaves have a sweetly pungent odor and can be used dry or fresh in cooking. A hot, sunny location with moist, rich, well-drained soil is ideal for sweet bay; but it will tolerate drought and stressful city conditions. It is rarely troubled by insects or diseases.

Leucothoe fontanesiana
Drooping leucothoe

Leaves 2 to 5 inches long, emerging leaves often purplish or bronze, maturing to lustrous dark green, bronzish or purplish in winter.

Zones 4 to 8.

Slow to moderate growth rate.

3 to 6 feet high, 3 to 6 feet wide.

In its natural habitat, this species is an understory plant found along stream banks and in shady woods. The species should be used in similar locations in cultivation. It forms such a dense tangle of stems that foot traffic through a large colony is almost impossible. Its growth habit is almost fountainlike, since the long, spreading, un-branched stems originate from the center of the plant and arch gracefully. The white, slightly fragrant flowers originate from the leaf bases but hang downward and are almost hidden from view. If used in unsuitable situations (dry, alkaline soils and windswept, sunny locations), this species fares miserably. Additionally, a severe leaf spot mars the leaves. A cool, acid, moist soil and shady location are pre-requisites for any measure of success in northern gardens. 'Girard's Rainbow' was selected for its striking new growth, which combines a mixture of white, pink, and copper. Eventually the leaves become green with whitish variegation. 'Nana' is a fine low-mounded form about 2 feet high and 6 feet wide, with lustrous dark green foliage. 'Scarletta' is a relatively new selection with lustrous dark green foliage, a more compact growth habit, and rich deep plum to purple winter color.

Leucothoe populifolia
Florida leucothoe

Leaves 1½ to 4 inches long, glossy rich green, new growth tinged red or purple.

Zones 7 to 9.

Moderate growth rate.

8 to 12 feet high, 8 to 12 feet wide.

Leucothoe fontanesiana

Left: *Ligustrum japonicum*
Below: *Magnolia grandiflora*

Florida leucothoe is one of the premiere evergreens for massing or screening in shady situations. The shrub is multistemmed, with long, lax, arching branches that give it a rather informal outline. Cream-colored flowers appear in May through June but tend to be lost under the foliage. The plant provides an excellent textural addition to the shade garden. Where possible, it should be blended with the rather stiff, formal rhododendrons and azaleas. It needs cool, moist, acid soil that is high in organic matter. Once established, the plant is self-perpetuating. It produces suckers that develop into wide-spreading colonies. Additional plants can be obtained by dividing a part of the colony. Florida leucothoe does not discolor in winter as *L. fontanesiana* does.

Ligustrum japonicum
Japanese privet

Leaves 1½ to 4 inches long, lustrous dark green.

Ligustrum

Zones 7 to 10.
Slow to moderate growth rate.
6 to 12 feet high, 6 to 10 feet wide.

Japanese privet is one of the most popular broadleaf evergreens because of its handsome foliage, wide soil tolerance, and pest resistance. Its growth habit is oval to rounded and dense, making it an excellent choice for hedges and screens. The creamy white, fragrant flowers occur in clusters 3 to 6 inches long in May or June. They are followed in September or October by blackish fruits that often persist through winter. This species is quite tolerant of dry soils, extreme heat, full sun, and moderate shade. Its only enemy is permanently wet soil. Japanese privet is used as a single specimen, for foundations, screens, hedges, and topiary, and in containers. 'Rotundifolium' is an exceedingly stiff, upright form, 4 to 6 feet high, with almost rounded leaves.

A closely related species, *L. lucidum* (glossy privet), is often confused with Japanese privet, but it is taller (20 to 25 feet), has larger leaves (3 to 6 inches long) and flower clusters (5 to 8 inches long), and blooms later (late June to July). Also, its leaves are not as glossy and the species is not as cold-hardy (zones 8 to 10) as Japanese privet.

Magnolia grandiflora
Southern magnolia, Bull bay

Leaves 5 to 10 inches long, polished waxy dark green above, either free of hairs below or covered with rusty brown hairs.

Zones 7 to 9.
Slow to moderate growth rate.
60 to 80 feet high, 30 to 50 feet wide.

This majestic evergreen maintains its dense pyramidal to oval outline into old age. As a specimen tree, it has no rivals among broadleaf evergreens and is best suited for that purpose. The fragrant, creamy white, 8- to 12-inch-diameter flowers appear in May or June and sporadically thereafter. The large rose red fruits (3 to 5 inches long) ripen in October, when their conspicuous orange red seeds become visible. The tree is somewhat messy, however, sporadically dropping flower petals,

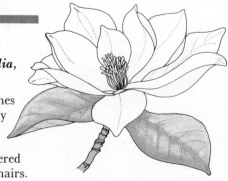

Magnolia grandiflora

Left: *Magnolia virginiana*
Below: *Mahonia aquifolium*

fruits, and leaves. It has no serious insect or disease pests. In northern areas the worst enemy is cold, which at −5° to −10°F will cause leaves to turn brown and stems to die back. Soils should be moist, acid, and well drained. Interestingly, southern magnolia can be grown in full sun or partial shade. Cold-tolerant cultivars include 'Edith Bogue', 'Samuel Sommer', and 'Victoria'. 'St. Mary' grows slowly to only 20 feet high.

Magnolia virginiana
Sweetbay magnolia

Leaves 3 to 5 inches long, lustrous dark green above, silvery beneath.
Zones 5 to 9.
Moderate growth rate.
20 to 30 feet high and wide, larger in the southern states.

The sweetbay magnolia is deciduous in cold climates. It is a rather wispy large shrub or small character tree that can be used most effectively around patios or in shrub borders or

groupings. The delightfully fragrant, creamy white flowers open in May through June and sporadically thereafter until September. This species must have moist, acid, well-drained soil. In alkaline soils, chlorosis will develop. Temperatures below 0°F usually result in defoliation.

Mahonia aquifolium
Oregon grape

Compound leaf composed of 5 to 9 leaflets, each leaflet 1½ to 3½ inches long, dull bluish green to lustrous dark green, usually tinged with or turning reddish purple in winter.
Zones 5 to 8 (zone 9 in the West).
Slow growth rate.
3 to 6 (sometimes 9) feet high, 3 to 6 feet wide.

Oregon grape is a steady, reliable shrub that seldom overwhelms a landscape. Bright yellow, slightly fragrant flowers appear in clusters 3 to 4 inches high and wide

during March or April and may be followed in August or September by waxy, bluish black, grapelike berries. The foliage is often a rich bronze when emerging, which adds interest to the landscape. Oregon grape combines well with other broadleaf evergreens and provides color and textural relief with rhododendrons and azaleas, especially in the winter months. Soils should be moist, acid, well drained, and high in organic matter. Chlorosis may develop in alkaline soils. Provide winter shade, since leaves tend to dehydrate.

'Compacta' is a dense, mounded selection with extremely lustrous dark green leaves and a bronze winter color. It grows 2 to 3 feet high and is hardy to −10°F. The leaves of 'Moseri' emerge orange to bronze red; they gradually change from rich apricot to apple green and finally dark green. 'Orange Flame' has blazing orange new foliage.

Mahonia aquifolium

Mahonia bealei
Leatherleaf mahonia

Each leaf is composed of 9 to 13 leaflets, each leaflet 1 to 4 inches long and 1 to 2 inches wide; dull dark to bluish green; leaf edges bear 5 to 7 prominent spines.
Zones 7 to 9.
Slow growth rate.
10 to 12 feet high, not as wide at maturity.

Leatherleaf mahonia is a bold, coarse-textured, rather clumsy-looking plant that becomes leggy

Nandina domestica

Nerium oleander

and open with age. When used against a brick building and underplanted with a suitable ground cover, it provides a beautiful textural effect. The lemon yellow, fragrant flowers appear at branch tips in February or March. Bees are fond of the flowers and serve as effective pollinators. The rich blue fruits (sometimes robin's egg blue) can be spectacular when they ripen in May or June. Leatherleaf mahonia prefers a moist, acid, rich, well-drained soil. It is excellent for use in heavy shade or full sun.

Nandina domestica
Nandina, Heavenly bamboo

Leaf composed of numerous leaflets, each leaflet 1½ to 4 inches long; entire leaf is rich metallic bluish green, often turning bronze or purplish in fall.

Zones 6 to 9.

Slow growth rate.

6 to 8 feet high, usually less in spread.

Nandina domestica

If the word *tough* could be applied to only one plant, it would most assuredly be given to *Nandina domestica*. Nandina thrives even under adverse conditions, and plants usually live to a ripe age without excessive coddling. Because it is often used as a hedge, the lovely flowers and fruits are removed in pruning. For best effect, nandina should be grouped or massed. It will become leggy if not pruned regularly. It resembles bamboo, and can be used to give an oriental look in

places where bamboo would not survive, or would be too invasive. Nandina is tolerant of drought and heat but not of extremely wet soils.

It grows well in full sun and moderate shade. The creamy flowers occur in 8- to 15-inch-long clusters during May or June and are followed in September or October by bright red fruits that persist through winter. 'Atropurpurea Nana' forms a 2-foot-high mound of curling leaves that turns rich red in cold weather. 'Harbour Dwarf' is a broad-mounded form that grows 2 to 3 feet high. Its leaves are only about half the size of those of other nandinas. It is a lovely, delicate selection useful as a ground cover or for massing.

Nerium oleander
Oleander

Leaves 3 to 8 inches long, leathery dark green.

Zones 8 to 10.

Fast growth rate.

6 to 20 feet high, usually slightly less in spread.

The flowers alone are sufficient reason to fall in

Nerium oleander

love with oleander; but its tolerance to salt, drought, heat, wind, and infertile soil makes it one of the most popular shrubs for western and southern gardens. The single or double flowers may be white, pink, rose, or red. They appear in June or July and continue into late summer and fall. Since flowers appear on new growth, overgrown plants can be pruned back in early spring if necessary. Oleander is used in highway median plantings in very sandy soil in Florida and in clay soil in California, which attests to its toughness. It makes an excellent screen, mass planting, or visual barrier.

Temperatures around 5° to 0°F will kill the plant to the ground.

Olea europaea

Osmanthus heterophyllus

Olea europaea
Olive

Leaves to 3 inches long, gray-green above, silvery beneath.
Zones 7 to 10.
Fast growth rate when young, slows with age.
20 to 30 feet high, similar spread.

Olea europaea is the famed olive of antiquity. A tender tree, it is grown in the Southwest and West commercially for its fruit and as an ornamental. The olive is well known for its gnarled, twisted trunk and branches and picturesque growth habit. It is ideally used as an accent or specimen plant, but it also makes a good hedge.

Olives thrive in hot, dry climates. They grow most vigorously when planted in deep, rich soil; but they are very tolerant of dry, shallow, alkaline or stony soils. Olives are easy to transplant; even old, established trees can usually be moved successfully. Olives have the disadvantage of producing great quantities of fruit, which create messy litter and readily stain pavement. 'Swan Hill' and 'Fruitless' are fruitless varieties. 'Skylark Dwarf' is dwarfed and fruits only lightly. Watch for scales and olive knot.

Osmanthus heterophyllus
Holly olive

Leaves 1 to 2½ inches long, lustrous dark green above, yellowish green beneath; prominent spines along leaf edges.
Zones 7 to 9.
Slow growth rate.
8 to 10 feet high, 8 to 10 feet wide.

Osmanthus heterophyllus

Holly olive is a dense, upright oval to rounded shrub that makes an excellent barrier, hedge, or screen. With age, the plant becomes more loose and open and the leaves lose their spiny margins. The plant requires essentially no pruning unless a formal hedge is desired. In October or November, tiny waxy white flowers appear at the bases of the leaves. The fragrance from the flowers on a single shrub can scent an entire garden. Holly olive is one of the few fragrant shrubs that blooms in the fall. It will grow in virtually any soil except one that is permanently wet. It is tolerant of drought and heat, and is free of insect and disease pests. 'Rotundifolius' is a slow-growing dwarf shrub with rigid, leathery, nonspiny leaves. Its branches have a wider spread than those of the species, and the ultimate height is about 5 feet. A closely related species, *Osmanthus* x *fortunei* (Fortune's holly olive), is a hybrid between *O. heterophyllus* and *O. fragrans* (fragrant holly olive). It may grow 15 to 20 feet high and resembles a haystack at maturity. The spiny-margined leaves are larger than those of *O. heterophyllus*. Similar fragrant waxy white flowers appear in October. This species is not as hardy and probably should not be used where temperatures drop below 0° F.

Pachysandra terminalis
Spurge, or Japanese pachysandra

Leaves 2 to 4 inches long, lustrous dark green throughout the seasons; new growth a rich yellow green.

Olea europaea

Pachysandra terminalis

Photinia × fraseri

Zones 4 to 8.

6 to 12 inches high, spreading indefinitely in loose, loamy soil.

There is no better ground cover for heavily shaded areas of the garden. It thrives in the shade of beeches, oaks, and maples and provides an unbroken, dense cover. Pachysandra spreads by rhizomes (underground stems), so the soil must be loose, friable, moist, acid, and well drained. Plants spaced 10 to 12 inches apart will fill in completely by the second growing season. Pachysandra can be used on the north side of houses, walls, and fences,

Pachysandra terminalis

where few ground-cover plants perform with any degree of certainty. It must have shade, because in full sun plants become yellow and lose vigor. Leaf blight and stem canker can be damaging, but vigorous plants are seldom troubled. The problem can be controlled by spraying.

'Green Carpet' is a new selection with darker green foliage and a more compact growth habit. 'Variegata' can be used to lighten dark areas of the landscape. The leaves are bordered with an irregular creamy margin, and the interior of the leaf is grayish green. It does not grow as vigorously as the species. Both selections are becoming more common in commerce.

Photinia serrulata
Chinese photinia

Leaves 4 to 8 inches long, lustrous dark green; new growth emerges rich apple green, bronze, to reddish purple.
Zones 7 to 9.
Fast growth rate.

20 to 25 feet high, 15 to 20 feet wide.

The Chinese photinia makes a rather handsome small tree or large shrub, especially when the lower branches are removed to expose the rich grayish black bark. The species can be used as a single specimen, in groupings, in corner plantings, and as a screen or hedge. In April, large flattish clusters of creamy white flowers appear at the ends of the branches. The odor is strong and unpleasant. Because of it, the plant should not be used near the house, especially near a bedroom window, for there would be no sleeping during the 2- to 3-week flowering period. Red fruits ripen in October and often persist through winter. This species is susceptible to fire blight and leaf spot. It does not tolerate very cold weather; 5° to 0° F will result in some leaf and stem injury. It is adaptable to extremes of soil and is tolerant of drought and heat.

A related species, Photinia x fraseri (Fraser photinia), is a hybrid between P. serrulata and P. glabra, Japanese photinia. Fraser photinia will grow 15 to 20 feet high, but it is generally more refined in habit and more tolerant of cold than P. serrulata. It also produces brilliant red new foliage in the spring. It is a popular plant and is used extensively for hedges and screens from zone 7 south. Entomosporium leaf spot has proven troublesome but can be controlled with proper fungicides.

Pieris floribunda
Mountain pieris

Leaves 1 to 3 inches long, deep dark green.
Zones 4 to 7.

Photinia

Pieris japonica 'Variegata'

Pittosporum tobira

Pieris floribunda

Slow growth rate.
2 to 6 feet high, similar or greater spread.
Mountain pieris thrives in cool climates and moist, acid, well-drained soils. It forms a neat, dense bushy outline with stiff branches. The white fragrant flowers occur in 2- to 4-inch-long dense upright clusters for 2 to 4 weeks during late March or April.

It is an excellent choice for the rock garden, foundation, or any place a neat, slow-growing evergreen shrub is required. In addition, it can be used under pines and other trees that provide a light shade. A fine selection is 'Millstream', more compact than the species, almost flat on top, and heavy flowering. Interestingly, neither the species nor 'Millstream' is troubled by the lacebug that affects Japanese pieris.

Pieris japonica
Japanese pieris

Leaves 1¼ to 3½ inches long, lustrous dark green; new growth emerges bronze or reddish.
Zones 5 to 8.
Slow growth rate.
9 to 12 feet high, 6 to 8 feet wide.
Pieris japonica forms a neat oval to rounded shrub with dense clustered foliage. The leaves appear to be tufted and emerge principally from the end of the stem.

The new leaves emerge with rich bronze or reddish tints before changing to lustrous dark green. The white to dark pink, urn-shaped, slightly fragrant flowers occur in 3- to 6-inch-long pendulous clusters from February to April. They are present for 2 to 3 weeks or longer, depending on the weather. Numerous selections have been made for foliage and flower color and for compact habit. The flowers are formed the summer prior to flowering; the pink- and red-budded forms are particularly attractive through the winter months. It makes an excellent companion shrub for rhododendrons and azaleas and can be successfully integrated in shrub borders or foundation plantings.
The Japanese pieris is quite adaptable and can be successfully grown over a wider geographic range than most other acid-loving plants.

It grows best in moist, rich, well-drained soils, but the only absolute requirement is good drainage. The only serious pest is the lacebug, which in the East has become devastating. The insect sucks the sap from the leaves, creating a yellowish, almost bleached plant.

Pittosporum tobira
Tobira, Japanese pittosporum

Leaves 1½ to 4 inches long, leathery lustrous dark green.

Pittosporum tobira

Prunus caroliniana

Prunus laurocerasus

Zones 8 to 10.

Slow growth rate.

10 to 12 feet high, 15 to 20 feet wide.

Japanese pittosporum is a lovely ornamental that is noted for its habit, foliage, floral fragrance, and adaptability. For foundations, massing, hedges, drifts under high shade, screens, and buffer or barrier plantings, the species has few peers. The creamy white flowers, which have an orange-blossom fragrance, appear in April or May. This popular plant adapts to both sandy and clay soils, if they are well drained. It thrives in full sun or moderate shade, tolerates salt spray, and can withstand a modicum of drought and heat. 'Variegata' has grayish green leaves edged with white. 'Wheeler's Dwarf' develops into a dense, compact spreading mound, ultimately reaching about 3 feet in height. It is excellent as a ground cover or for massing.

Prunus
The laurels

The *Prunus* group includes well over 200 species and many cultivars of trees and shrubs, including the stone fruits (peaches, plums, and apricots). The evergreen members of this genus, the evergreen laurels, are shrubs or small trees grown for their shiny green foliage. They bear creamy white flower spikes that are followed by red or purplish fruits. When crushed, the leaves and stems emit a distinctive fragrance reminiscent of almond extract; this fragrance is a characteristric of the genus and can be used to identify it. The evergreen laurels are used mainly as hedges, screens, and background plants; a few make attractive specimens.

Prunus caroliniana
Carolina cherrylaurel

Leaves 2 to 3 inches long, lustrous dark green,

margins smooth or with several spiny teeth.

Zones 7 to 10.

Fast growth rate.

20 to 30 feet high, 15 to 20 feet wide.

The typical plant is a small tree of dense, pyramidal to oval outline. As a single specimen, in informal groupings, or as a screen, it has much to offer. The fragrant whiteflowers are followed by lustrous black fruits in September that often persist into midwinter. The stems have a distinct maraschino cherry odor when bruised. Carolina cherrylaurel grows in soils ranging from virtually pure sand to clay. This particular species can become a weed because stray seedlings will germinate wherever birds fly. 'Bright 'n Tight' is a compact form with smaller leaves than the species and is probably a better choice for contemporary landscapes.

Prunus laurocerasus

Prunus laurocerasus
European or common cherrylaurel

Leaves 2 to 6 inches long, lustrous green.

Zones 6 to 9.

Moderate growth rate.

10 to 18 feet high, 25 to 30 feet wide.

The common cherrylaurel is best adapted to mild climates. The species is not widely planted in northern gardens; it is represented principally by the cultivars 'Otto Luyken', 'Schipkaensis', and 'Zabeliana'. The flowers are white and fragrant,

Pyracantha coccinea

Pyracantha koidzumii

and occur in cylindrical clusters during April or May. Purplish black fruits may follow. The real beauty lies in the lustrous dark green foliage. For foliage effect alone, it is the standard by which other broadleaf evergreens are judged.

Cherrylaurel requires a moist, acid, well-drained soil and shade. Plants will grow in full sun, but they are generally not as vigorous. In fact, cherrylaurel is one of the most shade-tolerant of all the broadleaf evergreens, ranking with Japanese pachysandra and English ivy for its tolerance.

The various cultivars can be used for massing, informal groupings, and hedges. They can also be used effectively in foundation plantings, especially where shade may present a problem.

'Otto Luyken' is a small, compact form with smaller leaves and flowers. It grows 4 to 6 feet high and wide and is hardy to zone 6. 'Schipkaensis' is the hardiest (zone 5) form. It grows 5 to 8 feet high and has a similar spread.

'Zabeliana' has narrow leaves and the finest texture of the three. It may grow 3 to 4 feet high and spread to 12 feet. It can be used as a ground cover in heavily shaded situations. It is hardy to zone 5.

Pyracantha coccinea
Scarlet firethorn

Leaves vary from ½ to 1½ inches long on flowering branches and to 2½ inches on nonflowering shoots, lustrous dark green, often becoming brownish in windswept or unprotected areas during cold winters.

Zones 5 to 9.

Fast growth rate.

6 to 18 feet high, variable spread.

This firethorn makes a spectacular show in fall when the abundant orange to red fruits are at their vibrant best. Firethorn is a large, wild, thorny shrub that will outgrow everything near it unless restrained. It is often trained against fences and walls. As a freestanding shrub, it can be spectacular, especially when several plants are scattered in loose groupings. It is also used as a hedge, but this treatment removes most of the flowers and fruits. The plant makes a good barrier or privacy screen because of the dense foliage and thorny stems. The white flowers appear in April or May and cover the entire plant.

Firethorn is troubled by mites, lacebug, and scab. Scab can be a serious problem on the fruits because it discolors them. Recent introductions with good scab resistance include 'Fiery Cascade', 'Mohave', 'Navaho', 'Rutgers', and 'Teton'. Several cold-hardy selections are 'Chadwickii', 'Kasan', 'Lalandei', and 'Wyattii'; but they are scab-susceptible.

Pyracantha coccinea

Pyracantha koidzumii
Formosa firethorn

Leaves 1 to 3 inches long, lustrous dark green.

Zones 8 to 10.

Fast growth rate.

8 to 12 feet high, 8 to 12 feet wide.

Formosa firethorn is a wild-growing, spreading shrub that tends to take over an area if left unchecked; the long

Quercus virginiana

branches appear to wander in all directions. It is excellent if espaliered on walls or buildings, or used in masses or groupings to hide unwanted objects or soften harsh architectural lines. The frothy white flowers appear in April or May, but the genuine beauty resides in the brilliant red fruits that ripen in September or October and often persist into spring. This species is more spectacular than *Pyracantha coccinea* but is less cold-hardy, often losing all foliage and suffering stem dieback at 0° F. It grows vigorously under good conditions but is tolerant of heat and drought.

Quercus agrifolia
Coast live oak

Leaves 1 to 4 inches, medium green, slightly glossy, spiny along leaf edges.
Zones 9 and 10.
Slow growth rate.
20 to 75 feet high, similar or wider spread.

The coast live oak is an integral part of the California coastal terrain, where it is native. The growth habit is massive, dense, somewhat rounded, and wide spreading. The heavy thick branches covered with dark gray bark grow in a twisting, picturesque manner, giving the tree a characteristic silhouette against the horizon.

When planting a live oak, give it plenty of room to grow. Although it grows slowly, it will ultimately attain great height and spread and requires a fairly large space to do it justice. Coast live oaks are mainly planted as street or shade trees. Culture of this magnificent tree outside its native habitat is not likely to succeed, as it is somewhat fussy and needs a mild Mediterranean climate. These trees need well-drained soil and will not tolerate any wetness around the base of their trunks. They are subject to root rot and are susceptible to several leaf-eating caterpillars.

Quercus virginiana
Southern live oak

Leaves 2 to 5 inches, lustrous dark green on upper surface, pale and slightly hairy on lower surface.
Zones 7 to 10.
Medium to fast growth rate.
40 to 60 feet tall, 50 to 120 feet wide.

To many, the southern live oak, with its branches festooned in Spanish moss, symbolizes the Deep South. It is native to the Southeast, where it is a popular and widely planted tree. The growth habit is mounding and wide spreading. The trunk is short and thick, and the branches grow horizontally, vsome almost touching the ground. They bear yellowish green catkins in spring that develop into acorns about 1½ inches long.

This long-lived tree is best used as a street tree or specimen in a setting where its size will not overpower the landscape. Southern live oaks prefer a sunny location and moist, fertile soil, but

Quercus agrifolia

they will grow in a wide variety of soils. Encourage fast growth by pruning, watering, and fertilizing regularly. Even as large trees, southern live oaks can be easily transplanted.

Raphiolepis umbellata
India hawthorn

Leaves 1 to 1½ inches long, leathery, lustrous dark green, may turn bronze or assume a purple tinge in winter.
Zones 7 to 10.

Raphiolepis umbellata

Rhododendron 'America'

Slow growth rate. 4 to 6 feet tall, similar spread.

This can be a wonderful low hedge, container plant, or mass planting. The habit is usually broad and mounded, although the shapes of cultivars vary; some are open and rangy, and others are dense and compact. The slightly fragrant white flowers appear in April, followed by purplish black berries in September that often persist into winter. India hawthorn prefers moist, well-drained soils but will tolerate some drought once established. Leaf spot, especially on plants in moist, shady areas, can be serious. Foliage injury is likely to occur when temperatures drop to −5° F.

Raphiolepis indica is closely related but is less hardy. The flowers are generally pink, although white forms do occur. Like *R. umbellata,* it flowers best in full sun, although it will produce a respectable show in partial shade.

Rhododendron
The rhododendrons

An extremely large group of plants comprising over 900 species and thousands of cultivars, rhododendrons are among the most popular garden shrubs. With proper selection, they can be grown from zones 3 to 9. Rhododendrons are used for every conceivable landscape purpose, but they are best in large groups, masses, naturalized settings, and in foundation plantings. A single rhododendron isolated in the landscape is definitely out of place.

The most important factor when selecting rhododendrons is to choose species that will tolerate your area's winter temperatures. Provide an open, well-drained, acid soil (pH 4.5 to 6.0) with an ample supply of organic matter. Maintain a cool, moist soil by providing partial shade and mulches. Use mulches also to reduce cultivation, which may damage the shallow, very fine, silky roots. Protect rhododendrons from drying winds and winter sun. Water thoroughly after transplanting and regularly thereafter. Also, rhododendrons use water in fall and winter and should be watered during these seasons. Remove old flower heads to stimulate flower bud formation for the following year.

Rhododendrons are susceptible to a host of diseases and insects; root rots and borers are the most severe. Good cultural practices reduce the incidence of disease.

Rhododendron species

RHODODENDRONS HARDY TO ZONE 3:

Rhododendron maximum
Rosebay rhododendron

Loose, open growth habit, 15 to 30 feet high, similar spread, purplish pink to rose flowers from June through July.

Raphiolepis indica

Left: *Rhododendron 'PJM'*
Below: *Sarcococca hookerana* var. *humilis*

RHODODENDRONS HARDY TO ZONE 4:

Rhododendron 'Boule de Neige'

Compact, rounded growth habit, 5 to 6 feet high, 8 to 10 feet wide, white flowers in May.

Rhododendron carolinianum
Carolina rhododendron

Rounded, open growth habit, 3 to 6 feet high with similar spread, light pink to deep rose flowers in May.

Rhododendron × laetevirens
Wilson rhododendron

Low, compact growth habit, 2 to 4 feet high, 2 to 6 feet wide, pink to pinkish purple flowers in May.

Rhododendron 'PJM'
PJM rhododendron

Rounded, dense growth habit, 6 feet high and wide, lavender pink flowers in April.

Rhododendron smirnowii
Smirnow rhododendron

Compact, broad, mounded growth habit, 6 to 8 feet high, rose pink flowers in May.

RHODODENDRONS HARDY TO ZONE 5:

Rhododendron catawbiense
Catawba rhododendron

Dense, rounded growth habit, 6 to 10 feet high, similar spread, lilac purple flowers in May through early June.

Rhododendron dauricum var. sempervirens
Dauricum rhododendron

Compact growth habit, 5 to 6 feet high, similar spread, rose purple flowers in March.

Rhododendron impeditum
Cloudland rhododendron

Cushionlike, compact growth habit, 12 to 18 inches high, 18 to 24 inches wide, purplish or bluish purple flowers in April through May.

Sarcococca hookerana *var.* humilis
Dwarf Himalayan sarcococca or sweetbox

Leaves 2 to 3½ inches long, lustrous dark green. Zones 5 to 8.
Slow growth rate.
1½ to 2 feet high, spreading indefinitely.
This plant offers a pleasant surprise for American gardeners because of the rich foliage, sweet-scented flowers, shade tolerance, and ease of culture. Dwarf sweetbox is a dense shrub that spreads by creeping stems to form a solid cover in heavy shade. Like *Pachysandra terminalis*, it is at the forefront of broadleaf evergreens for shady areas of the garden. The fragrant, small, whitish

Sarcococca hookerana var. *humilis*

flowers appear in March and are essentially masked by the foliage. When used as a low, billowy hedge or border along a woodland path, it provides a most enticing fragrance. It needs moist, rich, acid soil and grows best in a shaded location. There are no serious insect or disease pests. This plant should be considered when there is a need for a unique ground cover with excellent shade tolerance.

Skimmia japonica
Japanese skimmia

Leaves 2½ to 5 inches long, rich green and often lighter than most other broadleaf evergreens.

Left: *Skimmia japonica*
Below: *Vaccinium vitis-idaea*

Zones 6 to 8.
Slow growth rate.
3 to 4 feet high, similar spread.

The gardens of Europe are filled with this species, yet it is not well known in the United States. It is a beautiful, dense, mounded broadleaf evergreen shrub embodying excellent foliage, flower, and fruit qualities. In March or April, slightly fragrant creamy white flowers emerge from glossy maroon buds on male and female plants. The flower stalks are a rich maroon and provide interest before and after the flowers have

opened. On female plants, bright red fruits ripen in October and persist through winter, with some present into summer.

Japanese skimmia requires partial to full shade and rich, moist, acid soils. Protection from drying winds is also advised. It can be used effectively in groupings, shady borders, foundations, as a specimen plant, or simply as a large mass or unpruned hedge. Male and female plants are necessary for fruit set. Although spider mites are occasionally a problem, skimmia is usually free of insects and diseases.

Skimmia japonica

Vaccinium vitis-idaea
Mountain cranberry

Leaves ½ to 1 inch long, lustrous dark green, turning metallic mahogany red in winter.
Zones 3 to 5 (to 8 on the West Coast).
Slow growth rate.
10 inches high, slowly spreading indefinitely.

Vaccinium vitis-idaea

This species is a choice and cherished ground cover for cold-climate gardens, but it isrestricted to rock gardens and other small areas. The dainty white or pink flowers that appear in late spring are followed by conspicuous dark red fruits from ⅜ to ½ inch in diameter, ripening in September and October.

Soils should be cool, moist, acid, and well drained. Full sun to partial shade is acceptable. In winter, the foliage assumes a metallic mahogany red color.

Viburnum
The viburnums

The viburnum group includes a number of deciduous evergreens and shrubs, and occasionally small trees. The evergreen viburnums are grown for their lush foliage, pastel flower clusters, and attractive, sometimes unusually colored berries.

Viburnums are useful as hedges, foundation plants, screens, and accent plants. Most evergreen viburnums thrive in part to full shade and prefer rich, moist, well-drained acid soil. Some tolerate much drier, hotter conditions. Viburnums are relatively pest-free.

Virburnum davidii

Below: *Viburnum davidii*
Right: *Viburnum rhytidophyllum*

Viburnum davidii
David viburnum

Leaves 2 to 6 inches long, deeply etched with 3 veins, leathery, dark bluish green.

Zones 7 to 9.

3 to 5 feet high, 3 to 5 feet wide.

David viburnum forms a low, compact, dense mound of beautiful foliage that makes it suitable for foundations, groupings, massing, rock gardens, and accent use. The pink-budded flowers open to white, and occur in 2- to 3-inch-diameter clusters in April or May. The species requires male and female plants in close proximity to produce the rich blue fruits. Soils should be moist, acid, high in organic matter, and well drained. It is adapted to the Pacific Northwest, and in the East it is a delicate plant that requires careful cultivation. Protection from full sun and sweeping wind is necessary. It is a most beautiful broadleaf evergreen when properly grown.

Viburnum japonicum
Japanese viburnum

Leaves 3 to 6 inches long, almost leathery, waxy, lustrous dark green.

Zones 8 to 10.

Moderate to fast growth rate.

10 to 15 feet high.

A large, robust shrub, Japanese viburnum makes an excellent screen, hedge, informal mass, or background. The fragrant white flowers are produced in 3- to 4½-inch-diameter clusters during May. Red fruits may follow but are not reliably produced. It thrives in moist, fertile, well-drained soil in full sun or partial shade, but is quite adaptable. Temperatures below 10° F will result in leaf damage.

Viburnum odoratis-simum (sweet viburnum) is sometimes confused with *V. japonicum*, but grows taller (to 20 feet) and has a broadly pyramidal flower cluster. The leaves emit a disagreeable odor when crushed. It is probably less hardy than *V. japonicum* and is suitable for culture in zones 9 and 10.

Viburnum rhytidophyllum
Leatherleaf viburnum

Leaves 3 to 7 inches long, lustrous dark green and deeply wrinkled above, grayish to yellowish brown below, extremely hairy.

Zones 5 to 8.

Moderate growth rate.

10 to 15 feet high, 10 to 15 feet wide.

Leatherleaf viburnum is an excellent textural accent in any garden because of the bold, dark green leaves. It forms a large, upright arching shrub and requires much space. The yellowish white flowers appear in 4- to 8-inch-diameter clusters during May. The red fruits, which mature to black, will remain into November or December if not eaten by birds. This species requires cross-pollination for good fruit set; single plants are often disappointing.

Leatherleaf viburnum makes an excellent screen or shrub border addition, but it is most effectively used in groups of 3, 5, or 7 to break up open expanses of turf. In severe winters (−10° to −15° F) the leaves will be killed. The plant should be cut to the ground in late winter or

Viburnum odoratissimum

Left: *Vinca minor*   Below: *Vinca major*

early spring and will subsequently make 4 to 5 feet of new growth.

Viburnum x *pragense* resulted from a cross between *V. utile* and *V. rhytidophyllum*. It displays the best features of both parents. The lustrous dark green, 2- to 4-inch-long leaves are fully evergreen to −6° F. The habit is oval to rounded, with the branches uniformly distributed. It is a neater shrub than either parent and grows 8 to 10 feet high and wide. White flowers open in April or May; fruits are sparse. It has few peers for screening, groupings, foundation plantings, and shrub borders.

Viburnum suspensum
Sandankwa viburnum

Leaves 2 to 5 inches long, lustrous rich green.
Zones 9 and 10.
Fast growth rate.
6 to 12 feet high, 6 to 12 feet wide.
Sandankwa viburnum is frequently used for hedges, but it makes a rather attractive broad-spreading shrub if not restrained. It is popular in the Coastal Plain into Florida and on the West Coast. The white, faintly pink tinged, fragrant flowers occur in 2½- to 4-inch clusters. Reddish fruits follow but are seldom overwhelming. Although best suited to moist, fertile, well-drained soils, it is also adaptable to sandier, drier situations.

Viburnum tinus
Laurustinus

Leaves 1½ to 4 inches long, lustrous, almost black green.
Zones 8 to 10.
Moderate growth rate.
6 to 12 feet high, usually less in spread.
A fine plant for screens, hedges, and backgrounds, laurustinus offers excellent foliage, fragrant white flowers in late winter, and metallic blue-black fruits. The habit is distinctly upright to oval and dense. It prefers evenly moist, well-drained soil and full sun to partial shade. It withstands pruning and can be fashioned into topiary subjects. 'Eve Price' is a compact form with smaller leaves, attractive pink buds, and pinkish white flowers. 'Spring Bouquet' is a compact (6 feet) form with darker green leaves and rich pink buds opening to pinkish white.

Vinca minor
Common periwinkle

Leaves 1 to 1½ inches long, lustrous dark green throughout the seasons if sited in shade.
Zones 4 to 8.
Moderate growth rate.
3 to 6 inches high, spreading indefinitely unless confined.
Common periwinkle is second only to Japanese pachysandra in popularity as a ground cover. The lustrous foliage provides an ideal background for the 1-inch lilac blue flowers that appear like twinkling stars from March through May. It is a superb ground cover for heavily shaded

Vinca minor

gardens and even performs well in woodland situations. The soil must be loose, acid, moist, and well drained. Common periwinkle is extremely susceptible to drought stress. The trailing stems root as they come in contact with moist soil. It will fill in more rapidly than Japanese pachysandra. A canker that causes dieback in the crown area can be a significant problem but can be controlled with a suitable fungicide.

A closely related species, *Vinca major*, has larger leaves, stems, and flowers. It is more tender than *V. minor* (zones 7 to 9). The leaves may reach 3 inches in length; the bright blue flowers, 1½ inches in diameter; and the height, 12 to 18 inches. Uses and cultural requirements are similar to those of common periwinkle.

INDEX

Common names of trees are cross-referenced to general botanical-name listings. Numbers in **bold** indicate principal descriptions; numbers in *italics* indicate illustrations.

Climate Zone Map

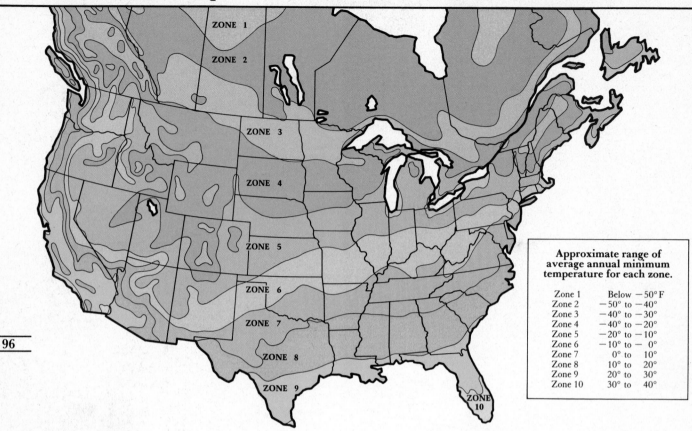

Approximate range of average annual minimum temperature for each zone.

Zone 1	Below −50°F
Zone 2	−50° to −40°
Zone 3	−40° to −30°
Zone 4	−40° to −20°
Zone 5	−20° to −10°
Zone 6	−10° to − 0°
Zone 7	0° to 10°
Zone 8	10° to 20°
Zone 9	20° to 30°
Zone 10	30° to 40°

Metric Chart

U.S. MEASURE AND METRIC MEASURE CONVERSION CHART

Formulas for Exact Measures   Rounded Measures for Quick Reference

	Symbol	When you know:	Multiply by	To find:			
Mass (Weight)	oz	ounces	28.35	grams	1 oz		= 30 g
	lb	pounds	0.45	kilograms	4 oz		= 115 g
	g	grams	0.035	ounces	8 oz		= 225 g
	kg	kilograms	2.2	pounds	16 oz	= 1 lb	= 450 kg
					32 oz	= 2 lb	= 900 kg
					36 oz	= 2 1/4 lb	= 1000g (a kg)
Volume	tsp	teaspoons	5.0	milliliters	1/4 tsp	= 1/24 oz	= 1 ml
	tbsp	tablespoons	15.0	milliliters	1/2 tsp	= 1/12 oz	= 2 ml
	fl oz	fluid ounces	29.57	milliliters	1 tsp	= 1/6 oz	= 5 ml
	c	cups	0.24	liters	1 tbsp	= 1/2 oz	= 15 ml
	pt	pints	0.47	liters	1 c	= 8 oz	= 250 ml
	qt	quarts	0.95	liters	2 c (1 pt)	= 16 oz	= 500 ml
	gal	gallons	3.785	liters	4 c (1 qt)	= 32 oz	= 1 l
	ml	milliters	0.034	fluid ounces	4 qt (1 gal)	= 128 oz	= 3 3/4- l
Length	in.	inches	2.54	centimeters	3/8 in.	= 1 cm	
	ft	feet	30.48	centimeters	1 in.	= 2.5 cm	
	yd	yards	0.9144	meters	2 in.	= 5 cm	
	mi	miles	1.609	kilometers	2-1/2 in.	= 6.5 cm	
	km	kilometers	0.621	miles	12 in. (1 ft)	= 30 cm	
	m	meters	1.094	yards	1 yd	= 90 cm	
	cm	centimeters	0.39	inches	100 ft	= 30 m	
					1 mi	= 1.6 km	
Temperature	°F	Fahrenheit	5/9 (after subtracting 32)	Celsius	32°F	= 0°C	
	°C	Celsius	9/5 (then add 32)	Fahrenheit	68°F	= 20°C	
					212°F	= 100°C	
Area	in.²	square inches	6.452	square centimeters	1 in.²	= 6.5 cm²	
	ft²	square feet	929.0	square centimeters	1 ft²	= 930 cm²	
	yd²	square yards	8361.0	square centimeters	1 yd²	= 8360 cm²	
	a	acres	0.4047	hectares	1 a	= 4050 m²	